THE FALKLANDS/
MALVINAS CAMPAIGN

THE FALKLANDS/ MALVINAS CAMPAIGN

A Bibliography

Eugene L. Rasor

Bibliographies of Battles and Leaders, Number 6
Myron J. Smith, Jr., Series Editor

Greenwood Press
New York • Westport, Connecticut • London

Library of Congress Cataloging-in-Publication Data

Rasor, Eugene L.
   The Falklands/Malvinas campaign : a bibliography / Eugene L.
Rasor.
      p.   cm.—(Bibliographies of battles and leaders, ISSN
1056–7410 ; no. 6)
   Includes index.
   ISBN 0–313–28151–3 (alk. paper)
   1. Falkland Islands War, 1982—Bibliography.   I. Title.
II. Series.
Z1945.R37   1992
[F3031.5]
016.99711—dc20   91–24365

British Library Cataloguing in Publication Data is available.

Library of Congress Catalog Card Number: 91–24365
ISBN: 0–313–28151–3
ISSN: 1056–7410

First published in 1992

Greenwood Press, 88 Post Road West, Westport, CT 06881
An imprint of Greenwood Publishing Group, Inc.

Printed in the United States of America

To
Cora, Jake, Hannah, Sam

CONTENTS

ACKNOWLEDGMENTS

A number of persons and institutions generously have provided assistance in the preparation of this historiographical and bibliographical survey of the Falklands/Malvinas campaign.

Emory & Henry College and its Faculty Enrichment Fund and the James Still Fellowship for Advanced Study from the Kentucky Scholars Program of the University of Kentucky have provided financial assistance and opportunities for research.

Appreciation is expressed to the following persons for support and assistance in a number of ways: Colin Baxter, Keith Bird, Alice Brown, Mickey Burris, James Casada, Barry Gough, the late Oron Hale, Robin Higham, Paul Kennedy, Roger Knight, the late Stephen Koss, the late Christopher Lloyd, Colby McLemore, Michael Moore, Wally Owen, Richard Pfau, Michael Puglisi, Bryan Ranft, Claire Rasor, Laura Rasor, John Roper, Dennis Showalter, Myron Smith, George Stevenson, Jon Sumida, Charles Sydnor, Joe Thompson, and David Woodward.

Likewise, appreciation is expressed to the following institutions for research assistance: in Great Britain, the British Library, Public

Record Office, National Maritime Museum Reading Room, Ministry of Defence Naval Library, the Institute of Historical Research at the University of London, the Portsmouth Public Library, and the university libraries of London, Cambridge, Oxford, Edinburgh, and East Anglia; in the United States, the Library of Congress and the George Marshall Library, Lexington, Virginia; in college and university libraries of Bowdoin, Chicago, Columbia, Duke, Emory, Emory & Henry, Furman, Georgetown, Harvard, Indiana, Kentucky, New York, North Carolina, Maryland, Old Dominion, Tennessee, Virginia, Virginia Tech, and Yale, and in libraries of the U.S. Naval Academy and the U.S. Naval War College at Newport, RI.

ABBREVIATIONS

AQDJ   ARMY QUARTERLY AND DEFENCE JOURNAL
BBC   British Broadcasting Corporation
HMSO   Her or His Majesty's Stationery Office
JRUSI   JOURNAL OF THE ROYAL UNITED SERVICES INSTITUTE
MP   Member of Parliament
NATO   North Atlantic Treaty Organization
NIP   Naval Institute Press
NIProc   PROCEEDINGS OF THE NAVAL INSTITUTE
NWCR   NAVAL WAR COLLEGE REVIEW
OAS   Organization of American States
RN   Royal Navy
RUSI   Royal United Services Institute
STUFT   Ships-Taken-Up-From-Trade
TEZ   Total Exclusion Zone
UP   University Press
VTOL or
VSTOL   Vertical Take-Off and Landing aircraft

THE FALKLANDS/
MALVINAS CAMPAIGN

PART I

NARRATIVE AND HISTORIOGRAPHICAL SURVEY

Chapter 1

INTRODUCTION

PURPOSE AND FORMAT OF THE BOOK

This book, a volume in the Bibliographies of Battles and Leaders series, is a comprehensive historiographical and bibliographical survey of the Falklands/Malvinas campaign of 1982. It is prepared as a reference and research guide for the use of all levels of scholars, students, and those interested in modern diplomacy, international relations, strategy, maritime and military operations, warfare in its broadest context, culture, and domestic politics, for example, in Great Britain, Argentina, and the United States.

In the formulation of this book the objective has been to incorporate all published books, monographs, oral histories, official histories and other governmental publications, dissertations, bibliographies, pertinent journal and periodical articles, anthologies, conference papers, and "culture," i.e., fiction, drama, art, videos, films, exhibitions, and postage stamps associated with the Falkland/Malvinas Islands and the military campaign. The languages of these published works are English, Spanish, German, and French. Sources appropriate to provide background information on the history, diplomacy, colonial development, international negotiations, and natural phenomena of the Falkland/Malvinas Islands are included.

Daily newspapers, Sunday newspapers and magazines, popular magazines and journals, and service journals have not been consulted nor has the coverage of any of those publications devoted to the Falklands/Malvinas campaign been incorporated in this bibliography. That alone would be a massive undertaking. The campaign generated much interest in the countries concerned and throughout the world. However, there is a section on journals, periodicals, magazines, and newspapers (chapter 11) which summarizes samples of some of the coverage. No effort has been made to conduct extensive research in these forms of publications.

Other publications which might contain items related to the Falkland/Malvinas Islands but are not included in the bibliography are works on nature, landscapes, seascapes, birds, animals, fish, mammals, agriculture, travel, and place-names. In the case of the Falkland/Malvinas Islands, stamps deserve a special place because they are a unique avocation for the Kelpers, the residents, and they have been used for political purposes by Argentina. The "Philatelic Factor" is covered in chapter 10.

The book is divided into two major parts for the convenience of the reader-researcher and user. Part I is the narrative and historiographical survey section which is subdivided into logical chapters, each with a short title. This half of the book describes salient events and related publications, integrating these factors into a coherent whole. One purpose of this narrative section is to make the campaign more understandable from a variety of perspectives and perceptions, British, Argentine, American, and Latin American. Various methodologies are incorporated, e.g., journalistic approaches, oral histories, academic surveys, political histories, and textbooks. Within this portion of the book there is description, evaluation, critique, assessment, qualification, and placement in context. Every entry found in the second section, the annotated bibliography, is integrated into the narrative and historiographical survey. Such processes of integration, analysis, and critical evaluation are the essence of historical inquiry. Such is historiography; thus, the historiographical survey. Scholars and students at all levels should benefit from it as a guide and reference aid.

In the narrative section, the first half, a conscious effort has been made to evaluate quality and identify important contributions. The process of critical analysis has been applied within each chapter and subsection. In most instances the best and most significant publications on the topic being discussed are described first and less important contributions are given less attention, usually later in the discussion.

The second half of the book, Part II, is the annotated bibliography, in which 554 works are numbered based on the last name of the author in most cases. Each entry is followed by extensive annotation providing a different form of detail and analysis from that found in the narrative and historiographical survey section. The annotation provides more specific and individual additional information about each of the publications, documents, and other resources available to the researcher. The bibliography is meant to be comprehensive.

For cross-referencing assistance, an item in the annotated bibliography is cited by number in brackets, e.g., [537], in the narrative and historiographical survey section every time that it is mentioned in that section. Such numbered citations in brackets are also found among the annotations themselves when appropriate. Two appendices are included: an extensive chronology which incorporates salient dates and important events associated with the Falklands/Malvinas campaign, and a glossary to further identify the most important persons. To provide additional assistance to researchers at every level, an index is added at the end.

HISTORICAL BACKGROUND OF THE CAMPAIGN

The terms selected to describe the events of the spring of 1982 in the South Atlantic Ocean area immediately stereotyped the bias of the user: "Falklands" for the British and sympathizers, "Malvinas" for the Argentines and supporters. Some resorted to the cop out "Falklands/Malvinas," and a few preferred "South Atlantic war." Some avoided the use of the term "war," opting for "conflict" or "campaign." It was the classic example of a limited engagement. After all, formal declarations of war were never made and both antagonists demonstrated maximum restraint. Nor has there been resolution or a peace settlement.

It was unusual in a number of ways. Max Hastings [229], one of the most respected chroniclers, called it "a freak of history" and confidently declared it to be the last colonial war that Britain would ever fight. Argentina had never fought an outside power before. Valerie Adams [3] noted that it was an unexpected type of war in 1982, "an anachronism." Jorge Luis Borges characterized the conflict as a quarrel between two bald men for possession of a comb! [99, pp. 459–64]. David Brown [61, p. 48] described the Falklands/Malvinas as "the islands which had always been on the front page of Argentine newspapers but on the back page of British atlases." Peter Beck [542, p. 124] has determined that the Falklands was number 242 on the list of priorities of the British foreign office.

Chapter 2

SOURCES

HISTORIES

Researchers at all levels might commence an investigation of the Falklands/Malvinas conflict with general histories of the antagonists, Argentina and Great Britain. Textbooks would be excellent places to acquire background information. A number of good ones are available.

Histories of Argentina which could be recommended included: David Rock, ARGENTINA, 1516–1982: FROM SPANISH COLONIZATION TO THE FALKLANDS WAR [433], updated in 1987; Donald Hodges, ARGENTINA, 1943–1987: THE NATIONAL REVOLUTION AND RESISTANCE [240]; and the NATIONS OF THE MODERN WORLD series on ARGENTINA by H. S. Ferns [153]. Ferns [154] also wrote the standard history of Anglo-Argentine relations in the nineteenth century. The primary issues then were investment, loans for development, rapid expansion, religion, and the Falklands/Malvinas. Susan and Peter Calvert, ARGENTINA: POLITICAL CULTURE AND INSTABILITY [78] and LATIN AMERICA IN THE TWENTIETH CENTURY [76], were published in 1989 and 1990 respectively. She has a South-ampton dissertation [79] and he was a professor at Southampton University. The Falklands/Malvinas campaign was not treated separately. Two essays, by David Feldman [152] in a journal and Roberto Alamann in ECONOMIC DEVELOPMENT ISSUES: LATIN AMERICA [102], introduced pertinent themes such as politicization of the armed forces and economic development, respectively, in the decades after World War II. The pertinent works of Robert Scheina [445,446,447], excellent general sources, will be cited elsewhere.

Choices of histories of modern Great Britain were more nu-merous. Some examples, particularly those with emphasis on the post–World War II period, included: Kenneth O. Morgan, THE PEOPLE'S PEACE: BRITISH HISTORY, 1945–1989 [363]; Walter Arnstein, BRITAIN YESTERDAY AND TODAY: 1830 TO THE PRESENT [13]; R. K. Webb, MODERN ENGLAND: FROM THE EIGHTEENTH CENTURY TO THE PRESENT [519]; and Glyn Williams and John Ramsden, RULE BRITANNIA: A POLITICAL HISTORY OF BRITAIN, 1688–1988 [525]. These were all widely acclaimed textbooks.

BIBLIOGRAPHIES

Searches for bibliographies wholly and exclusively devoted to the Falklands/Malvinas question and the campaign will not be satisfying. There has been nothing forthcoming in which all of the published literature on the topic has been collected, much less annotated and integrated.

Limited bibliographies have been produced. Margaret Laver [312] accumulated 1539 annotated entries on the islands and their dependencies in the 1970s. Sara de Mundo Lo [370] concentrated on exploration, discovery, and natural conditions of the islands with 23 titles of a total of 486 entries on the conflict. There was some annotation. A brief bibliography for cartographers on the Falkland/Malvinas Islands describing 50 examples of maps depicting the islands was by Angela Fordham [159]. Ruben Ramirez Mitchell [420] has a pamphlet, a selected bibliography on the Falklands/Malvinas.

Searches for sections of bibliographies devoted to the campaign will be productive. Garland Publishing's MILITARY HISTORY BIBLIOGRAPHIES series provided three pertinent volumes which included coverage of the Falklands/Malvinas campaign. BRITISH MILITARY HISTORY: A SUPPLEMENT TO ROBIN HIGHAM'S GUIDE TO THE SOURCES, edited by Gerald Jordan [277], included Barry Hunt's essay, "The Royal Navy since 1919" (pp. 317–43), there being several sources on the campaign listed. It is volume 10 of the MILITARY HISTORY BIBLIOGRAPHIES series. More sources and some analysis and narrative on the Falklands/Malvinas campaign can be found in Eugene Rasor, BRITISH NAVAL HISTORY SINCE 1815: A GUIDE TO THE LITERATURE; volume 13 of MILITARY HISTORY BIBLIOGRAPHIES series [421, pp. 453–61]. A third volume, number 12 in the MILITARY HISTORY BIBLIOGRAPHIES series, was by David LaFrance and Errol Jones, LATIN AMERICAN MILITARY HISTORY: AN ANNOTATED BIBLIOGRAPHY [308], with 12 chapters on the period from 1492 to the present.

Finally, there were some others of note: LA ARMADA ARGENTINA by Bernardo Eltzer [139] was a short bibliography of Argentine perspectives before and during the campaign; Everette Larson [310] assembled A SELECTIVE LISTING OF MONOGRAPHS AND GOVERNMENT DOCUMENTS ON THE FALKLANDS/MALVINAS ISLANDS OF THE LIBRARY OF CONGRESS, which included 149 monographs and 47 documents; and Peter Catterall [87] edited a new annotated bibliography of postwar British history with 15,000 entries.

REFERENCE

Reference compilations on and about the Falklands/Malvinas abounded. In reference areas of libraries and archives, look for official government publications, official documents, official investigations, atlases, various types of guides, and annual volumes collecting details of military/naval/air weaponry of the nations of the world. For purposes of researching the Falklands/Malvinas campaign the latter group will be most productive. A wide variety of excellent choices can be found.

Governments are constantly apologetic, i.e., they use every opportunity to state rationales and present their perspectives. Some call this propaganda. These publications are typically printed by government facilities and distributed widely as government documents. Libraries with extensive holdings display these types of documents in special collection areas.

British government departments and Parliament produced a number of official documents directly related to the conflict. The British Central Office of Information published THE FALKLANDS ISLANDS AND DEPENDENCIES [501] in March 1982 and in September BRITAIN AND THE LATIN AMERICAN INDEPENDENCE MOVEMENTS [502]. The timing of the first may have been accidental but that of the second obviously was not. The same year the Foreign Office put out THE FALKLAND ISLANDS: THE FACTS [505].

Raphael Perl [397] compiled a documentary sourcebook, published in 1983, containing 52 documents, including treaties and diplomatic papers, and a bibliography citing 274 articles, all published before the conflict. There were two information guides on the Falkland Islands by Ian Strange [473,474], who was an agriculturalist.

Two pages of coverage, "The Recapture of the Falkland Islands, 1982," were included in A WORLD ATLAS OF MILITARY HISTORY, 1945–1984 by Tom Hartman and John Mitchell [227, pp. 86–87]. There was a chronology and maps of the islands and the region.

Annual compilations of all of the weapons of each of the nations of the world fill sets of shelves in the best libraries. Surprise at the outbreak of this conflict led to interested parties on both sides and at all levels, professional military, intelligence, journalistic, and "buffs," scrambling for their JANE'S or other annual collections on military forces of the world. A hasty look at one of these excellent military, naval, and air warfare annuals such as JANE'S FIGHTING SHIPS [268], JANE'S ALL THE WORLD'S AIRCRAFT [267], or COMBAT FLEETS OF THE WORLD [101] would immediately provide the reader with reliable information on the general capabilities of the opposing forces. JANE'S, of course, was a British publication, but it was just as informative about the forces available to Argentina. It has been widely acclaimed as extraordinarily authoritative and reliable. COMBAT FLEETS was the French publication FLOTTES DE COMBAT in English translation. The 1982/83 edition (published in 1981 in France) devoted pages 4–15 to Argentina and pages 219–72 to Great Britain, in a total of 890 pages. COMBAT FLEETS included details on warships, aircraft, and weapons systems whereas JANE'S published three separate annual publications on warships, aircraft, and weapons systems. JANE'S included editorials and tended to be more critical of British authorities for neglecting the armed forces, e.g., "this wholesale emasculation of the Royal Navy's ships and support" (from the 1983–1984 edition, p. 133). There were also JANE'S ALL THE WORLD'S AIRCRAFT [267] and a new publication for 1981–1982, JANE'S NAVAL REVIEW [269]. The latter analyzed the campaign in "The Lessons of the Naval War in the Falklands" by John Moore (1982–1983 edition, pp. 14–23). A source not available in 1982 but later quite enlightening on the weaponry of the antagonists was the NAVAL INSTITUTE GUIDE TO WORLD NAVAL WEAPONS SYSTEMS [376].

Another useful reference guide was CONWAY'S ALL THE WORLD'S FIGHTING SHIPS, 1947–1982 in two volumes [104]. This one actually covered the campaign (vol. 1, pp. 128–29). CONWAY'S described the rapid assembling of the task force as "a masterpiece of speed and efficiency" and the campaign as one in which "numerically inferior forces had repeatedly out-thought and out-fought the opposition." In the section on Argentina (pp. 393–99) the navy was described as involved in political activities and as unprepared for the Falklands/Malvinas invasion, having had no advanced warning. The German version, with German-English translations, of these annual compilations was WEYER'S WARSHIPS OF THE WORLD [523], first begun in 1900. The 55th, 1980–1981 and 56th, 1982–1983 editions were applicable for information about the fleets which participated in the campaign.

Some excellent reference sources focused on particular types of ships. For the Royal Navy, which interested parties undoubtedly investigated, there were John Moore, WARSHIPS OF THE ROYAL NAVY [358] and J. J. Colledge's [98] historical index of all British ships from earliest times, incorporating 14,000 entries in

two volumes. For the Moore volume, originally published in
1979, there was an updated edition in 1981; for the Colledge
volume the latest edition was 1969 and it has subsequently been
updated and expanded during the late 1980s, now including
24,000 entries. Roger Chesneau presented AIRCRAFT CARRIERS
OF THE WORLD [92], a catalogue of specifications of all aircraft
carriers. This could be another source from which information
could be learned about important Argentine and British warships.

Fewer sources were available about the Argentine armed forces. They had never fought an outside power. Indeed, during
the past decades they had frequently fought themselves. A look
at JANE'S or an equivalent would divulge the fact that Argentina
possessed modern and sophisticated ships, aircraft, weapons, and
forces, including an aircraft carrier, modern jet attack planes,
EXOCET missiles, submarines, helicopters, and mine warfare
capabilities. These publications would be available to anyone
with access to a good library. As seen above, more extensive and
detailed information would be available about the British forces.

Excellent sources of information for research purposes were
published reports of studies and investigations. There have been
several, most of them official, of the preliminaries and the activities of the Falklands/Malvinas campaign. These were discrete
investigations with specific purposes and with separate rationales. Each will be elaborated upon below. A list of them using
brief titles is as follows:

- Lord Shackleton I (1975–1976) [452] and II (1982) [453]
- Lord Franks [168]
- Beach [27]
- Information and Media [249, 250]
- BELGRANO [252]
- Rattenbach Report of Argentina [422]
- Several House of Commons studies [248, 249, 250, 251,
  252, 253]

Chapter 3

GEOGRAPHY

EXPLORATION OF THE SOUTH ATLANTIC
AND BRITISH IMPERIALISM

The Falkland/Malvinas Islands are located in the South Atlantic Ocean 340 miles northeast of Cape Horn, about 300 miles east of the Argentine coast, and 3300 miles south of Ascension Island, the closest base available to the British. There are the two large islands, East and West Falklands, and about 340 smaller islands. They are wild and unspoiled, inhabited by penguins and sheep and about 1800 "Kelpers," the name given to the local inhabitants.

Dispute has continued about the earliest discovery of these islands and the associated dependencies. The English and Spanish claimed to have discovered them in the sixteenth century. Appendix I, the chronology, has sorted out some of the numerous conflicting claims. The thesis of Enrique de Gandia [188] was that Duarte Barbosa discovered the Falkland/Malvinas Islands. A purely Argentine perspective on early claims, including extensive documentation, was contributed by Laurio Destefani [545] a year before the campaign. Enrique R. Guinazu [213] published a beautifully illustrated survey which fully covered Argentine claims.

There were others. The famous French explorer Louis-Antoine de Bougainville [55, 56] was said to be an early discoverer during voyages in the 1760s. The name Malvinas came from this occasion: the French sailors originated from St. Malo on the French side of the English Channel, thus LES ISLES MALOUINES, which was hispanicized into LAS ISLAS MALUINAS, the Malvinas Islands. An original account was by Antonie Pernety [398], published in three volumes in French in 1769 and in English in 1787.

Edward J. Goodman [201] published a history and a bibliography of the exploration of the South American area; the latter included 919 entries. THE GEOLOGY OF THE FALKLAND ISLANDS, including scientific reports of the British Antarctic Survey, was by Mary Greenway [207]. V. F. Boyson [57] has a geographic history with an annex devoted to its natural history by Rupert Vallentin.

An extraordinary and fateful detailed cruising guide to the coasts and inlets of the Falkland/Malvinas Islands was formulated in the 1970s by an experienced yachtsman-Royal Marine officer, Ewen Southby-Tailyour, during a tour of duty with the Marine guard. He participated in the campaign and his manuscript was used for the British planning phases of the amphibious and other operations. It has since been published [466].

Great Britain attained the status of imperial hegemony over much of the world during the eighteenth and nineteenth centuries. In the diplomatic and the military controversies associated with the Falklands/Malvinas, much was made of imperialism, colonization, and decolonization. The decolonization process began immediately after World War II and was effectively completed in the 1960s. The Falkland/Malvinas Islands were a British colony. To learn more of these imperial and international issues, the researcher should go to sources on imperialism. Some examples included Bernard Porter, THE LION'S SHARE: A SHORT HISTORY OF BRITISH IMPERIALISM, 1850–1983 [409]; Andrew Porter and A. J. Stockwell, BRITISH IMPERIAL POLICY AND DECOLONIZATION, 1938–1964 [408]; A. P.

Thornton, IMPERIALISM IN THE TWENTIETH CENTURY [481]; and an article by J. P. Taylor, "Argentina: The Falklands and Colonialism" [478].

As the Yale University historian Paul Kennedy [287] has repeatedly pointed out, economics, finance, commercial activity, and maritime endeavors were the basis of British imperialism and naval mastery. Argentina was, of course, never a British colony, but the characteristics of informal empire definitely applied. Economic factors were presented, albeit in obsolete form, in James Rippy, BRITISH INVESTMENTS IN LATIN AMERICA, 1822–1949: A CASE STUDY IN THE OPERATIONS OF PRIVATE ENTERPRISE IN RETARDED REGIONS [432]. For Argentina, as pointed out by H. S. Ferns [154], British investments accelerated beginning in the 1890s and reached a peak in 1934. At that time they comprised about one-tenth of the total of British capital and one-third of all of it in Latin America. During the post–World War II period, the islands and dependencies increasingly became a drain on British economic resources. That was confirmed in SHACKLETON I [452].

The British did sponsor an extensive economic assessment of the islands and surrounding region in 1975—the Shackleton study, headed by Lord Shackleton. He was a former Labour MP and son of the Antarctic explorer, Sir Ernest Shackleton. ECONOMIC SURVEY OF THE FALKLAND ISLANDS, two volumes, was published in 1976 [452]. The report described a degenerating, demoralized, and impoverished society in which the Falkland Island Company and absentee landlords were exploiting the situation. The study group determined that the current economy was overwhelmingly dependent on wool production, there being 650,000 sheep at that time. Potential for development of oil and fish resources should be investigated. That was SHACKLETON I [452]. The Argentines objected to the study and precipitated certain diplomatic crises by threatening British ships at sea. The British recalled their ambassador. Martin Honeywell of the Latin American Bureau [243] and Richard Johnson [274] wrote on these issues. Immediately after the 1982 campaign, a second study, SHACKLETON II, was conducted and published in September [453]. This report concluded that the dispute over sovereignty limited the potential for future economic development.

REGIONAL ISSUES, THE DEPENDENCIES, AND ANTARCTICA

For administrative, cartographic, and diplomatic reasons, Great Britain has chosen to combine the Falkland/Malvinas Islands with their "dependencies," South Georgia and South Sandwich, and to associate those with British Antarctic Territory, South Orkneys, South Shetlands, and other islands in the South Atlantic. South Georgia, 700 miles east of the Falklands/Malvinas, played a large role in the campaign. It was the site of the preliminary incident which the Argentines expanded into invasion of the Falklands/Malvinas. Robert Headland [231] published a book on South Georgia, including aspects of its history, geography, commercial activities, and military actions.

Head'and [230] has also compiled a comprehensive and useful listing of Antarctic expeditions. Over 3000 ventures were reviewed, beginning in 700 BC until 1988, number 3342 being the meeting of the Antarctic treaty nations in 1988. Vivian Fuchs, OF ICE AND MEN: THE STORY OF THE BRITISH ANTARCTIC SURVEY, 1943–1973 [179], recounted a series of British expeditions, the first being a naval operation with subsequent ones evolving toward more scientific endeavors. D. G. Sherrard [454] rode along during an annual voyage of the Royal Navy through areas around Antarctica in the early 1980s. He described his observations.

Over the past decades an elaborate international treaty-conference system has evolved formulating agreements on all scientific, exploration, commercial, and military activities of Antarctica and surrounding regions. The first Antarctic Treaty was concluded in 1959, going into effect in 1961. Twenty-two nations signed. The Falklands/Malvinas campaign has upset these fragile arrangements but this basis could provide a possible solution to the sovereignty question. Peter Beck [38,40,43] has analyzed these issues.

The first volume of Albert Norman, THE FALKLAND ISLANDS, THEIR KINSHIP ISLES, THE ANTARCTIC HEMISPHERE AND THE FREEDOM OF TWO GREAT OCEANS: DISCOVERY AND DIPLOMACY, LAW AND WAR [383], has been published. It covered the naval and land phases of the campaign.

THE NAVAL BATTLE OF THE FALKLANDS, 1914

For many naval history buffs, "The Falklands" signified the occasion for one of the few decisive naval battles of World War I. The battle of Coronel had been fought off Chile along the western coast of South America on 1 November 1914; the German Far Eastern squadron annihilated a British squadron of older ships. Two cruisers and 1600 men were lost. The Admiralty under Sir John Fisher rushed reinforcements to the Falkland/Malvinas Islands to deal with the Germans, and on 8 December 1914 the two forces met as the British squadron (which, this time, included two new battle cruisers, one named INVINCIBLE) annihilated the Germans. The Germans lost two cruisers and 1900 men.

The best general naval survey of the period was by Arthur Marder, FROM "DREADNOUGHT" TO SCAPA FLOW: THE ROYAL NAVY IN THE FISHER ERA, 1904–1919 [329], the detailed accounts of Coronel and the Falklands being in volume 2. Others included Henry Newbolt [378], Robert Keith Middlemas [343], and Hector Bywater [543].

The Falklands battle has been the focus of several studies: CORONEL AND THE FALKLANDS by Barrie Pitt [402]; a volume in the BRITISH BATTLES series by Geoffrey Bennett [47]; by T. D. Bridge [60]; by J.J.C. Irving [265]; an early one by A. Neville Hilditch [235]; an assessment of the battle and its aftermath by Henry Spencer-Cooper [468]; by Harold Hickling [234], who was a sailor at Coronel and the Falklands; by the prolific Edwin P. Hoyt [256]; and by Richard Hough [246] and Hans Pochhamer [405], both from the German perspective. The Falklands battle has also held prominent places in other surveys: an older summary of major naval battles by Barry Bingham [51]; in volume 1 of Winston Churchill, WORLD CRISIS [94]; and in Richard Plaschka [404], who reviewed a number of naval battles during the first two decades of the twentieth century, including Coronel and the Falklands.

Allan Millett edited the three-volume MILITARY EFFECTIVENESS [346], a systematic investigation of military and naval actions, the first volume covering World War I. The Falklands battle was cited as the last naval battle fought by gunfire alone and without the cramping tactical effects induced by mines, torpedoes, submarines, and aircraft. That is disputed. The battle of the River Plate of December 1939, early in World War II, against the German pocket battleship, GRAF SPEE, was fought under identical conditions when none of those innovations was present. It was fought in waters nearby to the Falklands/Malvinas and off the Argentine coast.

Chapter 4

POLITICS

THE POLITICAL SITUATION IN ARGENTINA

Argentina gained its independence from Spain early in the nineteenth century. Its political history has been unstable and cyclical, with periods of military rule and dictatorships followed by efforts at reform and democratic governments. Much has been written about the military and Argentine politics. Guillermo Makin [327] reviewed these issues for the century 1880 to 1982.

Most decisive in post–World War II Argentine history was the regime of Juan Peron. Peron first came upon the scene in 1943 when he was involved in a military coup ousting President Ramon Castillo. In 1946 he was elected president, serving until his exile in 1955. A powerful political movement, the Peronist party, was built up. Peron returned to power in 1973, died in 1974, and was replaced by his wife, Isabel. She was expelled in 1975.

In "Argentina: The Departure of the Military—End of a Political Cycle or Just Another Episode?," Alain Rouquie [437] reviewed past military regimes as if they occurred in cycles: the Peronists, then 1966–1973, and most recently, 1976–1983. The consequences were economic collapse, interservice rivalry, and "the tragic adventure in the South Atlantic." Rouquie took the opportunity to condemn the United States for treachery and Great Britain for its "inordinate reaction," the counter-invasion.

During that cycle of military dictatorship in effect at the time of the campaign, the Junta in control in the late 1970s ruthlessly repressed opposition in what was sometimes called "the dirty war." Thousands of people were arrested and thousands more "disappeared." A group of Brazilian bishops estimated the number of disappeared at 7300; an important group, Mothers of the Plaza de Mayo, claimed the number was closer to 30,000. Amnesty International and others vehemently condemned such actions and the military regime. "Argentina's Dirty War" has a recent chronicler, Iain Guest [212]. Andrew Graham-Yooll, a journalist opposed to the war, recalled the "disappeared" in A STATE OF FEAR [204]. The regime of General Jorge Videla ended in December 1981 and was replaced by a military Junta headed by Army General Leopoldo Galtieri.

The Argentine Junta consisted of Galtieri, Admiral Jorge Anaya, and Air Force General Arturo Lami Dozo. General Galtieri had been openly courted by the U.S. administration of President Ronald Reagan, one objective being to gain approval and participation of Latin American states in intervention in Central America. In December 1981, shortly after becoming president, Galtieri was invited to the United States and was entertained by cabinet ministers Caspar Weinberger and Jeane Kirkpatrick, among others. Argentina had announced an intention to become actively involved in support of U.S. activities in Nicaragua. Presumably it was such diplomatic activities and offers of military and other forms of aid which led the Argentine Junta to assume that the United States would not oppose military initiatives over the Falklands/Malvinas question. Marshall Van Sant Hall wrote ARGENTINE POLICY IN THE FALKLANDS WAR: THE POLITICAL RESULTS [507] for the U.S. Naval War College.

When it comes to the subject of the Falklands/Malvinas, all of the various Argentine regimes have consistently whipped up mass hysteria and irredentism, playing up xenophobic passions. This was recovery of Argentine territory, noted Julius

Goebel [199]. Juan Moreno wrote LA RECUPERACION DE LAS MALVINAS [362] in 1973.

Murray Kempton [286] presented General Galtieri's case and claimed that Galtieri had modelled himself on the Italian dictator Mussolini, hoped for a cheap victory, and vowed to fight to the last man. LOS NOMBRES DE LA DERROTA by Nester Montenegro [354] touted interviews with officials including "a fundamental protagonist" who may have been General Galtieri. There were no startling revelations.

Elsewhere in this annotated bibliography (Chapter 5, "The 'Signals' "), the matter of "signals" is mentioned in several contexts. Interestingly, under this category of Argentine politics, LA PRENSA [309], the influential Buenos Aires newspaper, possibly was conveying "signals" on two occasions. On 24 January and 7 February 1982, LA PRENSA published articles to the effect that if the current bilateral negotiations taking place in New York City broke down, Argentina would resort to force.

Some Argentines appeared to have been just as surprised as many British that the invasion took place when it did and that the British reaction was so extreme. In a review of the Argentine literature, Simon Collier [99] summarized some explanations by Argentines on why the British responded so soon and so violently to the invasion: a Protestant-Catholic or a North-South antagonism, future potential for oil, and even a suspected menopausal state of the British prime minister! Interestingly, some cited the events of the spring of 1982 as the "first" Malvinas war, there being obvious anticipation of further conflicts over the sovereignty issue. Adolfo Perez Esquivel, recipient of the Nobel Peace Prize of 1980, supported the invasion "for historic, legal, and geographical reasons" [199, p. vii].

Perhaps more common was the book of Eugenio Ravenal, ISLES OF DISCORD: A FILE ON THE FALKLANDS [423]. Ravenal quoted Patrick Henry! "We have done all we can to avert the storm. . . . We must fight!" In his review of the background he insisted that Argentina had succeeded to the territorial rights of its mother country, Spain.

There was opposition to the campaign within Argentina. Roberto Roth wrote DESPUES DE MALVINAS, QUE . . . ? [436, p. 12] after the campaign, calling it "an obscene parody of patriotism,"

but he does praise air force pilots—none of them were "fat brigadiers." He referred to events as "the First Malvinas War."

Two movies produced during the war by Juan Jose Jusid,
LA ROSALES [281] and ASESINTO EN EL SENADO DE LA
NACION [280], were allegories critical of events in 1982 by
recounting stories of past scandals and notorious neglect by
officers of their men. These dramas were meant to raise the
consciousness of contemporary Argentines.

THE POLITICAL SITUATION IN GREAT BRITAIN

Government in Great Britain was the original parliamentary
democracy, and support for the decision for counter-invasion
was surprisingly strong. The majority of the British people and
their representatives in Parliament, Conservative, Labour and
other parties supported the war effort. Most decisive and most
determined of all was the prime minister, Margaret Thatcher.
She headed the Conservative party which had been in power
since 1979. Early in 1982 the fortunes of her party appeared to
deteriorate. Much was made then and later of the "Falklands
factor," the influence of the campaign on party politics.

Political opinion before and during the conflict can be determined by reviewing the extensive PARLIAMENTARY DEBATES:
HANSARDS [393 and 394], for the House of Commons and House
of Lords. This involved searching dozens of volumes to extract
pertinent portions of debates dealing with the Falklands/Mal-
vinas question over several decades. Conveniently, a compilation has been formulated by the government printing office. A
DIGEST OF DEBATES IN THE HOUSE OF COMMONS, 2 APRIL
TO 15 JUNE 1982 [247], reviewing six occasions of debate and
many parliamentary questions and statements, was published in
book form for sale.

Noel Annan [8] reviewed "Mrs. Thatcher's Case," the rationale
of the British position, in the NEW YORK REVIEW OF BOOKS. In
a BBC interview [25] in late April, Thatcher stressed the right of
self-determination of the people of the Falklands as an important
consideration. Hugo Young, a perceptive journalist, has written
three biographies of Margaret Thatcher [535, 536, 537], including

THE IRON LADY, a name for her originated by the Russians in 1976, about the time she took over as Conservative leader. Patrick Cosgrave [109] described the "First Term" of the Thatcher government, the period from elections in 1979 to 1983, chapter 7 (pp. 179–210) being pertinent on the campaign. Another account of the first term was by Nicholas Wapshott and George Brock [515]. Other political and personal biographies were by Dennis Kavanagh [284, 285], Chris Ogden [390], Robert Skidelsky [456], Penny Junor [279], and Peter Jenkins [270]. Titles included MAGGIE; THATCHERISM, THE END OF CONSENSUS?; and THE ENDING OF THE SOCIALIST ERA.

The majority of the British public and members of the House of Commons from all parties supported the war. However, there did develop a vocal and articulate radical opposition to "Mrs. Thatcher's War." Among the leaders were Tam Dalyell [115, 116, 117], Anthony Barnett [20, 21], Anthony Arblaster [9], and Tony Benn [46].

In an article [20] and book [21] entitled IRON BRITANNIA, Anthony Barnett observed that the war gave "a virulent new lease on life to Margaret Thatcher's authoritarian populism" [article, p. 1]. Barnett was writing for the NEW LEFT REVIEW during the closing days of the campaign. He reviewed the history as he saw it: the conflict was a "repeat of a repeat"—the Falklands operation of 1833 and the Suez crisis of 1956—and there were chapters on "Churchillism" and the "crackpot Parliament." Lawrence Freedman [171] assessed Barnett's critique as better organized than that of Tam Dalyell.

That outspoken and sensational critic and radical member of Parliament wrote three books on the Falklands era, ONE MAN'S FALKLANDS, THATCHER'S TORPEDO, and MISRULE [115, 116, 117]. The titles suggested particular outrage over the sinking of the Argentine cruiser, BELGRANO, but he accused the government of welcoming the Argentine invasion as a device to divert attention from domestic problems. Dalyell called the BELGRANO attack "an act of naked aggression" perpetrated specifically to quash efforts at a negotiated settlement. Dalyell has twice been suspended from the House of Commons for calling Thatcher "a bounder, a liar, a deceiver, a cheat, and a crook." Dalyell's role will be elaborated upon elsewhere.

Anthony Arblaster wrote of THE FALKLANDS: THATCHER'S WAR; LABOUR'S GUILT [9]. Tony Benn, an outspoken leader of the Labour party who openly opposed the war, has published his views [46].

History Workshop, a kind of radical and academic think-tank, sponsored a three-volume piece on PATRIOTISM, edited by Raphael Samuel [442]. The essays were stimulated by the chagrin and disappointment some radicals felt because the anti-war effort had failed so miserably. To them it seemed the country had gone mad: militarism, war rhetoric, and the language of 1066 AND ALL THAT, an outlandish spoof. They noted the parody and mockery of the cheers sending off a task force of a shrunken navy desperately scraped together to do battle with a Third World military Junta. In a review by Neal Ascherson [15, p. 3], Peter Jenkins of the GUARDIAN called it "Parliament's war!" "After it is all over, the bad British government had contrived to float itself off the rocks on a raft of jingoism."

There had been several internal efforts in Great Britain prior to 1982 to seek a solution. In 1968 the Labour Foreign Secretary, Michael Stewart, initiated such an attempt, but to no avail. Two Labour Members of Parliament, Colin Phipps and John Gilbur, took a tour of the Falklands in 1975. They concluded that it would be impossible to exploit the economic potential without Argentine cooperation. Colin Phipps [401] wrote of the investigation.

In a more sensational domestic political episode, in 1980 Conservative minister of State at the Foreign and Commonwealth Office Nicholas Ridley made a study-visit to the Falklands and returned to report to the House of Commons, reminding them of the recommendations of the SHACKLETON REPORT [452] of 1976 and touting a lease-back proposal. The islands had been "blighted" by the sovereignty dispute with Argentina. The Falklands Lobby, comprising Falkland Island Company interests and representatives for the "Kelpers," mobilized backbenchers and others in opposition. Ridley was mercilessly "mauled" in the House and the proposal was dropped. It was clear that the Falklands question was a very hot political issue, presumably to be avoided at all costs. Peter Beck [39, 40] analyzed these concerns.

THE "KELPERS"

Domestic information about the people of the Falkland Islands, called "Kelpers" from the seaweed which was prolific in the region, can be found in the local newspapers, the older GAZETTE [146], started in 1891, and the more recent JOURNAL [147], both published in Port Stanley. Examples of articles included information about explorers, fishing, whaling, sealing, the royal visit of 1973, and Antarctica. There was a fact-book printed early in 1982, THE FALKLAND ISLANDS: THE FACTS [145].

The Falklands Lobby was mentioned frequently. That was a pressure group backed by the Falkland Island Company which was influential in London and in Parliament. G. M. Dillon [129] contended that it mostly represented company, East Falkland, and managers' interests and not those of West Falklands and non-managers.

An Argentine perspective on the economy, development potential, and the Kelpers was published in two books by Haroldo Foulkes [161, 163]. The first Shackleton mission, SHACKLETON I [452], and prospects for oil were discussed.

"Self-determination and the Falklands" by Denzil Dunnett [134] reviewed one of the more important issues in the dispute. Thatcher insisted that that was a decisive factor; "Let the people decide," she proclaimed. Dunnett questioned whether the population should have been considered "a people" in this matter.

John Smith, 74 DAYS: AN ISLANDER'S DIARY OF THE FALK-LANDS OCCUPATION [459], was the memoir of a 25-year resident-employee of the British Antarctic Survey. This account depicted Kelper feelings, e.g., resentment over each of the concessions negotiated for cooperation and coordination with Argentina such as medical treatment, air service, and communications—"driving in the wedge," Smith called them.

Chapter 5

DIPLOMACY

THE FALKLANDS/MALVINAS QUESTION

Over the years leading up to the crisis of 1982 a number of options with the objective of resolution of the long-term diplomatic dispute were discussed and placed on the table. Examples of possible solutions included the usual decolonization process, associated statehood, United Nations trusteeship, third party guarantees, functional integration, lease-back, condominium, and compensation. One major obstacle was the issue of self-determination of the residents, the Kelpers.

The question of sovereignty and disputes and claims concerning the Falkland/Malvinas Islands can be traced back to the sixteenth and seventeenth centuries. Appendix I, the chronology, presents pertinent episodes of these early developments. The noted literary expert, Samuel Johnson, wrote THOUGHTS IN THE LATE TRANSACTIONS RESPECTING FALKLAND ISLANDS [275] in 1771, circulating copies to members of Parliament. He reviewed Spanish claims of the previous two centuries.

"Title to the Falklands-Malvinas under International Law" by Jeffrey Myhre [373] reviewed pertinent episodes relating to disputed claims before 1833. "The Falkland Islands Crisis of 1770: Use of Naval Force" by Nicholas Tracy [492] recounted an intervention which forced the Spanish to withdraw from the islands fifty years before the 1830s. Comparing several diplomatic studies, Julius Goebel [198, 199] concentrated on pre-1811 events when the role of England was minor.

In a review essay, Walter Little [320] focused on the roles of Great Britain, Argentina, and the United States, the dispute over sovereignty, and the failure of attempts at peacemaking. G. M. Dillon [129] of the University of Lancaster analyzed political events leading up to the conflict. For about two decades there were some efforts and suggestions to resolve the dispute: transfer of sovereignty, functional integration (i.e., cooperation and coordination with the Argentines), condominium (i.e., joint sovereignty), trade-off (cede outlying islands), and lease-back. The Kelpers insisted on self-determination. A sovereignty dispute degenerated into war. Peter Beck [542] reviewed the Dillon piece and assessed the results of the Falklands/Malvinas campaign in a 1991 article. The Calverts [74, 77, 79] emphasized the period at the turn of the twentieth century; both Goebel and the Calverts agreed that international law was irrelevant in this case.

Other writers included Philip Windsor [528] on the diplomatic dimensions; Peter Calvert in three instances [74, 75, 77]; J.C.J. Metford [339]; and Fritz and Olga Hoffmann [241], all of whom insisted the primary dispute was over sovereignty.

Peter Beck has devoted much research to this issue. He published a review of the dispute, "A Search for a Way Forward, 1968–1981," in February 1982 [39], just before the invasion. He noted then that these types of territorial and/or sovereignty disputes have been difficult to resolve because positions have hardened. Beck later published a review of the international aspects [40]. He pointed out that the dispute had been active since 1833 and there were key doubts as to the legal status as of January 1833. General Galtieri and the Argentines certainly saw January 1983, the 150th anniversary, as the ultimate date for action. The secret and determined resolve of the new Junta when it was installed in December 1981 was to finally "settle" the Falklands/Malvinas question by 1 January 1983. That date appeared frequently for internal consideration and even on occasion, although not explained, for external use in the Argentine media.

A number of noted authorities have produced informative reviews of the diplomatic background: Lord Carrington, the British foreign minister who resigned in April 1982 demonstrating his failure to anticipate Argentina's invasion, which he called Britain's "national humiliation," wrote his memoirs [86]; Patrick Cosgrave [108] produced a biography of Carrington, "the Fall" being covered in chapter 2 (pp. 16–41); Francis Pym [419], Carrington's successor as foreign minister, noted various constraints and opportunities in an address to Chatham House; Sir Nicholas Henderson [232], British ambassador to the United States, wrote of his views and participation during the crisis for the ECONOMIST; Sir James Cable wrote for ENCOUNTER [72]; former minister of foreign affairs of Argentina, Dr. Bonifacio del Carril [85], wrote in late April 1982; and British diplomat Robert Andrew Burns [67] reviewed British efforts as an academic researcher in 1985.

National and international private foundations and agencies, often called "think-tanks," and international conferences have focused on the issues of the conflict. The Royal Institute of International Affairs [438] produced a survey by academic specialists while the dispute was in process. SIPRI, the Stockholm International Peace Research Institute, produced a review [471] and sponsored a study by Jozef Goldblat and Victor Millan [200]. Goldblat and Millan stressed that the dispute stimulated the arms build-up, especially because of the failure to resolve the issue.

For the Institute for the Study of Diplomacy of Georgetown University Douglas Kinney [291] reviewed the origins, nature, and chronology of the crisis and attempts at settlement: "radicalization of decolonization," negotiations, third-party mediation, shuttle diplomacy, and intervention by the Security Council and secretary general of the United Nations. There were catchy titles: "urgent signals," "final signals, intended or not," "the Lobby," and the Central American connection. THE FALKLANDS WAR: LESSONS FOR STRATEGY, DIPLOMACY, AND INTERNATIONAL LAW, edited by Alberto Coll and Anthony Arend

[97], was an anthology of 15 papers presented at an international conference assembled in the fall of 1982 at the University of Virginia law school. The papers were on diverse topics and of unequal value, some obviously written in haste by non-experts and some appropriately by recognized scholars. Subjects included boundary disputes, Antarctica, the Organization of American States, and laws of war. "The Falklands Conflict" was the subject of a conference at the University of Keele in September 1990. Contributions included those by former Falklands Governor Sir Rex Hunt and General Sir Jeremy Moore, the British land commander. The proceedings were edited by Alex Danchev [544] and will be published in 1992.

The diplomatic-historical version favorable to the British interpretation was by Mary B. R. Cawkell [88, 89]. She discounted the Spanish claim based on prior discovery. Various agencies of Parliament and the government published several apologies, rationales, and information pieces: those of the Foreign and Commonwealth Office [503, 504, 505, 506] included one entitled ARGENTINE MISINFORMATION: BACKGROUND BRIEFING, which accused the Argentines of propaganda-mongering, and the Central Office of Information [500], published a collection of documents.

Lowell Gustafson wrote on the diplomacy of the conflict in a book [215] and in a University of Virginia dissertation [216]. He concluded Argentina had a superior historical claim but the British stressed the principle of self-determination.

The diplomatic history most cited by the Argentines and condemned by the British was that of Julius Goebel [198, 199], published by Yale University Press in 1927, followed by a Spanish translation in 1950 and a reprint in 1982. After reviewing many of the salient incidents, Goebel finally concluded that the solution was a matter of power. Similarly, the Argentines most often cited Ricardo R. Caillet-Bois [73], whose extensive use of documents and comprehensive analysis were quite persuasive. Originally published in the late 1940s, it, too, was reprinted in 1982. Annegret Haffa [217] linked the Beagle Channel dispute with Chile and the Falklands/Malvinas conflict.

On the Argentine side, cases were made by a number of writers. Camilo Barcia Trelles published EL PROBLEMA DE LAS ISLAS

MALVINAS [18] in 1943, reprinted in 1968. Causes, perspectives, and solutions were reviewed by Ricardo Becu, INGLATERRA PROMETIO ABANDONAR LAS MALVINAS [44], in 1975; Alfred Bologna [53] in an article in 1983; and Oscar Luis Viola [512]. In 1950 Jose Arce published LAS MALVINAS: LAS PEQUENAS ISLAS QUE NOS FUERON ARREBATADAS [10], translated the next year as THE MALVINAS: OUR SNATCHED LITTLE ISLES [11]. The islands had belonged to Argentina since 1810, well before the British occupation of 1833. The basis of that claim was "jus gentium." Federico Melendez [336] reviewed the international confrontation. In Spanish and in English editions, Admiral Laurio Destefani [127, 128] reviewed British imperialism and illegal invasions of previous centuries and insisted that "the Malvinas are Argentine" (p. 5) because of inheritance from Spain, because Argentines had been illegally expelled, and because of proximity and geography. "We will never give them up from the 1833 attack, nor will we ever do so!" In two other historical surveys, one before and one after the campaign [545, 546], Destefani presented extensive details and documents supporting the Argentine position. As early as April 1982, Osiris Troiani [494] reviewed the diplomatic preliminaries and some suggested solutions, e.g., "Hong Kong" and "Mission Rowlands."

A German analysis of the conflict was written by Hermann Weber [520]. Gregory Treverton and Don Lippincott [493] wrote a summary for the Pew Program foundation of Pittsburgh.

The matter of sanctions, comparatively not so important in 1982, has been investigated nevertheless. Military and economic sanctions were implemented against Argentina, for example by the European Community and the United States. Margaret Doxey [133] has a general essay and M. S. Daoudi [118] a specific one. Both Argentina and Great Britain seized each other's assets during the dispute. The Argentines did place the accumulated interest for British banks in escrow in New York.

Victor Bulmer-Thomas [64] of the University of London edited a recent (1989) assessment of British–Latin American relations: they have not been good, especially since the high level of economic and commercial relations of the nineteenth century have decreased. The Falkland/Malvinas campaign set them back much further. The essayists, including Bulmer-Thomas, indicted the British government for, among other things, sending the wrong signals, failing to make timely, courageous decisions about the disposition of the Falklands, and forgetting the importance of anniversaries. They also praised as the best effort at post-war analysis Michael Charlton's book, THE LITTLE PLATOON [91], a summary of eight broadcasts for BBC Radio Three during the summer of 1987. An impressive listing of interviews was incorporated: Nott, Pym, Lewin, Shackleton, Haig, Kirkpatrick, Henderson, Weinberger, Vernon Walters, and high-ranking Argentine participants.

THE UNITED STATES

Whether they wanted to be or not, the United States was immediately drawn into the Falklands/Malvinas dispute. It presented a serious dilemma to the Americans. The United States had a long history of friendly relations with both antagonists and was anxious to continue them.

Unlike the previous crisis over the Suez Canal in 1956, the British enjoyed the active and generous assistance of the United States. In the Suez case, the British and the French were forced to withdraw in a most humiliating fashion. Relations between the United States and Britain remained strained for some time after Suez.

In the Falklands/Malvinas case, the British enjoyed access to American assistance in the form of weapons, logistics, intelligence, communications, and base facilities. Primarily responsible for the rapid and expanded U.S. direct assistance to Great Britain was Caspar Weinberger, secretary of defense of the United States. In his memoirs, FIGHTING FOR PEACE [521], "Cap" described how he alerted all U.S. forces to respond immediately to all British requests for assistance, e.g., aircraft fuel; missiles, especially Sidewinders; bases, notably Ascension Island; and intelligence. He saw the motivations of the Argentine Junta as primarily designed to distract the attention of the Argentine people away from economic and political problems.

A former secretary of the navy, John Lehman, wrote COMMAND OF THE SEAS [316], which included an appraisal of the

Falklands/Malvinas conflict. The United States provided substantial logistical assistance, communications facilities, and intelligence information. There were important lessons for the United States, e.g., appreciation of the quality of military training and high motivation of British personnel.

The most significant first-hand recollections in this regard were those of Alexander Haig in CAVEAT: REALISM, REAGAN, AND FOREIGN POLICY [218]. Haig was secretary of state and he led an extensive and elaborate shuttle-diplomacy effort during the last days of April 1982. Those efforts failed. Sir Nicholas Henderson first brought information of potential crisis on 28 March. What followed, Haig described [218, p. 261], was "a case study in miscalculation, national rivalry, war fever, and the way in which the leaders of nations can be driven by the most basic human emotions toward fateful decisions." Haig candidly exposed disputes he had with the White House staff and especially with Jeane Kirkpatrick, U.S. ambassador to the United Nations. Secretary of defense Caspar Weinberger supported Haig, and even more enthusiastically and openly supported British military efforts. Haig finally concluded that this crisis brought him down as secretary of state and he ultimately blamed the White House staff, especially James Baker, later secretary of state himself.

As was to be expected, Jeane Kirkpatrick has presented her views, in an article [294] and in two books [292, 293]. Her priority was maintenance of good U.S.–Latin American relations. The press tried to fit the conflict into traditional East-West tensions, she said, but it was more appropriate to categorize it under the old world-new world analogy. She praised the Charlton oral history [91], for which she had been interviewed.

Chaim Kaufman [283] reviewed this as a case study of shuttle diplomacy. Secretary of state Haig insisted that the United States remain neutral at first and undertook an effort at shuttle diplomacy during late April, travelling back and forth from London to Buenos Aires to Washington and around again. This ended in failure, Haig announcing on 30 April that the United States was tilting in favor of Great Britain.

A number of observers, especially from Argentina, blamed the United States for the entire problem, e.g., Alain Rouquie [437] and Elisabeth Reimann [428] who recalled the Monroe

Doctrine. The most extreme claims about machinations of the
United States were made by three Argentine journalists, Oscar
Cardoso, Ricardo Kirschbaum, and Eduardo van der Kooy, in
FALKLANDS: THE SECRET PLOT, translated by Bernard Ethell
[82]. Their original purpose was "a certain unpublished history of
the war" (p. iv), which, upon further investigation, unfolded as
a "plot" hatched by the United States in Washington among the
highest members of the Reagan administration, including Alexander Haig, Jeane Kirkpatrick, Caspar Weinberger, Richard Allen,
and, especially, Vernon Walters. Most of these, the journalists
contended, were involved in a famous luncheon in 1981 honoring
General Galtieri at the Argentine embassy. This was part of a plan
directly to involve Argentine armed forces in Reagan administration operations in Central America. After becoming president
of Argentina, Galtieri was again entertained in Washington,
this time by Vice President George Bush, in December. Allen
had publicly described Galtieri as "a majestic personality" and
Weinberger saw him as "very impressive." These journalists
purported to publish (pp. 81-89) the full phone conversation
between Reagan and Galtieri at 10 pm on 2 April 1982 when
Reagan tried to persuade Galtieri not to invade. Overall, this
was a sensationalist, simplistic, narrow view strictly from the
Argentine perspective. There was much on the role of the United
States and virtually nothing on British aspects.

Peter Calvert reviewed U.S.–Latin American relations during
the crisis [75]. The role of the Organization of American States
(OAS) in the Falklands conflict was the focus of a study by Gordon
Connell-Smith [103]. John Moore [359] assessed the viability of the
OAS in relation to the Falklands/Malvinas crisis and concluded
that the system, the oldest regional organization, failed in this
instance. An OAS resolution condemned Great Britain and urged
support for Argentina.

THE UNITED NATIONS

The permanent representative of the United Kingdom to the
United Nations, Sir Anthony Parsons [395], recalled developments associated with his duties in New York during 1982.

In February bilateral negotiations were taking place in New York. Then, suddenly, and with absolutely no warning, the incident involving the scrap metal workers on South Georgia occurred: "There seemed to be more interest in it at the U.N. than any event ever before. . . . [There were] hundreds of press and TV interviews." He then recalled mobilizing the efforts to get Security Council Resolution 502 passed on 3 April: 10 votes for, Panama against, and 4 abstentions. That achievement was one of the most impressive in U.N. history.

Raul Labougle [301] in 1965 and Gunnar Nielsson [382] in 1988 wrote on aspects of the dispute and the United Nations.

THE "SIGNALS"

One "game" which diplomats play relates to overt or covert acts of one government at odds with another government. These events are supposed to convey certain intentions not obvious or not directly related to the actions themselves. This often happened when a government was about to change long-standing positions or redirect its activities. Such actions were sometimes called "signals." Already noted above (p. 21), for example, LA PRENSA's [309] two articles published months before the invasion threatened some future resort to force. Was that a "signal" from the Junta aimed at the British government, a direct warning of an anticipated change in the Argentine diplomatic stance?

Much has been made of various "signals" allegedly given by the British government indicative of potential intentions on matters related to the Falklands/Malvinas question. Recall that the British had been engaged in the decolonization process for forty years and that the Falkland/Malvinas Islands, a colony, might be next in the continuing process. The colony was remote, isolated, and an economic burden to Great Britain. The first SHACKLETON REPORT [452] openly admitted the liabilities. Peter Beck [38] observed that there were several signs during the 1970s that the British were losing interest in the South Atlantic region generally.

The FRANKS REPORT [168] stressed the factor of "signals." The point was that actions of the British government conveyed inclinations or indications, overt or covert, diplomatic or colonial, to Argentina that interests and intentions related to the South Atlantic region were in the process of change. Presumably the feeling was that perceptive Argentines should exploit these changes. Two notable examples were HMS ENDURANCE and an aspect of British citizenship.

HMS ENDURANCE represented the final consistent presence of official British forces in the South Atlantic region. It had been announced that her deployment was to be terminated. That decision had been made earlier, but the Foreign Office convinced the Ministry of Defence to delay the withdrawal precisely because of the fear of "signals" to be interpreted by Argentina. Her removal could clearly be seen as an overt act signifying change in British interests if not outright full abandonment of obligations in the region. The Defence Review of 1981 [352] provided for the permanent withdrawal of ENDURANCE.

Incredibly, Admiral Sir Edmund Irving, former hydrographer of the Royal Navy, wrote "Does Withdrawal of ENDURANCE Signal a Falklands Desertion?" for GEOGRAPHICAL MAGAZINE in January 1982 [264]. He noted the upcoming 150th anniversary of British colonization and presented details on ENDURANCE, a converted Danish commercial ship. The elder Shackleton's ENDURANCE had been lost in 1915. For Irving, withdrawal of this ENDURANCE sent wrong signals to Argentina. Michael Socarras [463] wrote of "signals" and Phil Williams [526] saw a number of "miscalculations."

The second "signal" concerned the matter of British citizenship, a volatile issue in domestic politics and among British Commonwealth states and former colonies for decades. The disposition of Hong Kong, for example, has been much debated during the 1980s, as the lease of that territory expires in the 1990s and Hong Kong reverts to China. In 1981 the British government passed a Nationality Bill providing that some inhabitants of these states and dependencies would automatically be offered full British citizenship. The Kelpers, the 1800 residents of the Falkland/Malvinas Islands, would not be granted such preferred status.

Chapter 6

THE FORCES

THE ARGENTINE FORCES INVOLVED

The armed forces of the two belligerents of the Falklands/Malvinas conflict now require review. As noted above, detailed information about military, naval, and air forces of 160 countries of the world can be found in annual compilations such as JANE'S [267, 268, 269] and COMBAT FLEETS [101]. Other sources were surveys and histories of these forces covering specific periods of time. There were several of these devoted to Argentine and British forces. For Argentina, it was its navy which has been studied most. Unfortunately, other Argentine forces have not been well served with historical surveys.

General background on four Latin American navies was provided by Frank Pandolfe [392] in a Tufts dissertation. For 500 years, Latin American naval forces have been decisive power-brokers in intercontinental, intracontinental, and domestic conflicts. Fernando Milia [344] wrote of the Argentine navy in 1990.

Best and most comprehensive about the Argentine navy were the works of Robert Scheina, historian of the U.S. Coast Guard.

Scheina has contributed significantly at several levels: his LATIN AMERICA: A NAVAL HISTORY, 1810–1987 [445] was the definitive work, comprehensive and scholarly. There were two chapters devoted to the Falklands/Malvinas campaign. Scheina also reviewed Latin American navies after the war [446] and the Argentine navy for JANE'S NAVAL REVIEW [444]. Finally, there were three additional articles in the PROCEEDINGS [447, 448, 449]. Scheina has conducted extensive research in Argentina, and he was obviously sympathetic to their position. He played down the claims that the Junta acted to divert attention from domestic problems. There had been years of intense irredentist frustration and the Junta was persuaded with justification that the British would concede the islands without a fight. There were articles on the navy's Super Etendards [448] and on Argentine submarine operations [449]. The latter was most informative. The submarine SAN LUIS did attack two frigates on 10 May, but the torpedoes missed. SAN LUIS and SANTA FE had participated in amphibious landings and other operations earlier. If only the Argentine junta had waited until the time of the original planned invasion. Then there would have been more Super Etendards (probably a dozen more), more EXOCETS, more time to get French experts to properly install and prepare the EXOCETS, more aviator training, and perhaps more modern German- designed submarines which were anticipated soon. These were all further demonstrations that the Falklands/Malvinas campaign could have gone either way.

THE BRITISH FORCES INVOLVED

Argentine forces have been poorly served with analytical historians other than Dr. Scheina; the British forces, especially the Royal Navy, have enjoyed a plethora of attention. The British action, Operation Corporate, was primarily a naval and Royal Marine endeavor with assistance from the merchant marine. The best and most recent history of British maritime forces was Paul Kennedy, THE RISE AND FALL OF BRITISH NAVAL MASTERY [287], a comprehensive survey of all of the factors, especially economic, imperial, and strategic, influencing British naval and maritime developments in modern times. The equivalent for the British army was Correlli Barnett, BRITAIN AND HER ARMY, 1509–1970: A MILITARY, POLITICAL, AND SOCIAL SURVEY [22]. James Ladd [303] recalled a long list of operational activities of the past in the authorized history of the Royal Marines in 1980. Surveys for longer historical periods have been formulated by Max Arthur [539] for airborne forces and John Strawson [544] for the army. A review essay by Hew Strachan [472] critiqued significant writings and writers on "The British Way in Warfare Revisited": Sir Michael Howard, Paul Kennedy, and Correlli Barnett.

Most of the other writing to be reviewed in this section has concentrated on the post–World War II era and the transformation from a great power, a winner of World War II, to the status of a dependent force which has suffered a series of debilitating reductions and demobilizations. Another aspect of the transformation has been the consolidation and integration of the armed forces of Great Britain under the Ministry of Defence. Earl Mountbatten was instrumental in facilitating the restructuring of the armed forces. The best description of the post–World War II reorganization of the Ministry of Defence was by Franklyn Johnson [273]. Mountbatten, who served as chief of the Defence Staff for six years, wrote the foreword.

The general studies of this period have included those of Michael Dockrill [132], who summarized British defence policy after World War II, including the Sandys White Paper of 1957, and the "Way Forward" or "Nott" program of 1981, the two decisive defense reviews calling for "draw-downs" of British armed forces. These were individually presented: Wyn Rees [425] on the Sandys review and the official program by the Ministry of Defence [352]. Other defense assessments were by William Snyder, THE POLITICS OF BRITISH DEFENCE POLICY, 1945–1962 [461] and a Princeton dissertation [462]; James Wyllie, THE INFLUENCE OF BRITISH ARMS [533]; and Dan Smith, THE DEFENCE OF THE REALM IN THE 1980s [457].

A distinguished list of naval analysts have produced a large number of surveys. A well-known academic, Geoffrey Till of King's College, London, and the Royal Naval College, Greenwich, has written and edited several general assessments, some being anthologies of high level strategy conferences: THE FUTURE OF BRITISH SEA POWER [483], which ended with pessimistic conclusions; MODERN SEA POWER [485], which covered everything from cod wars to nuclear wars; MARITIME STRATEGY AND THE NUCLEAR AGE [484], which included an essay on the Falklands campaign by Till in the second edition (1984); and BRITAIN AND NATO'S NORTHERN FLANK [482], which stressed other primary obligations of British forces. Till called the Falklands campaign the world's most serious naval war for forty years and a very public war because of the inordinate interest in it.

Keith Speed's memoirs, SEA CHANGE: THE BATTLE OF THE FALKLANDS AND THE FUTURE OF BRITAIN'S NAVY [467], was an extraordinarily candid and refreshing evaluation of the recent past and future of the Royal Navy by the first lord of the Admiralty who spoke out against the 1981 "Nott" cutbacks and was fired. The office of first lord was subsequently dropped.

The list of distinguished naval writers continues. Admiral J. R. Hill has written four surveys, THE ROYAL NAVY: TODAY AND TOMORROW [239], BRITISH SEA POWER IN THE 1980s [237], MARITIME STRATEGY FOR MEDIUM POWERS [238], and AIR DEFENCE AT SEA [236], each of which was profusely illustrated and informatively narrated. These were realistic assessments of the transition from an independent to a dependent force. There were others: Antony Preston, HISTORY OF THE ROYAL NAVY IN THE TWENTIETH CENTURY [412]; John Woods, a pseudonym, "The Royal Navy since World War II" [531]; Desmond Wettern, THE DECLINE OF BRITISH SEAPOWER [522]; and Philip Pugh, "Maintenance of Post-War British Sea-Power" [418]. Pugh cited the Harrier VSTOL as the most significant technical innovation.

Sir James Cable, a prestigious diplomat and naval writer (sometimes under the pseudonym Grant Hugo), completed BRITAIN'S NAVAL FUTURE [71] just before the spring of 1982 and added "Preface and First Thoughts on the Falklands" (pp. ix-xvi). Cable was obviously depressed over the cuts of the 1981 Defence Review but saw some hope that public interest and consciousness were now raised. Cable also wrote a review of the diplomatic developments for ENCOUNTER [72].

Somewhat less impressive was the contribution of Richard Humble, THE RISE AND FALL OF THE BRITISH NAVY [259]. In a consistently shrill fashion, Humble lamented that a force which took four centuries to develop and perfect could be demolished in four decades. He indicted all post–World War II governments, Conservative and Labour. Now (1986) the Thatcher government was refusing even to replace ships lost in the Falklands/Malvinas campaign. Humble then listed three priorities of the 1980s, interestingly not including a nuclear strategic deterrent which he denounced as "luxury," "machismo," and distracting from the needs of conventional security. The book was mostly cold war rhetoric and Earl Mountbatten–bashing.

SEA POWER IN THE FALKLANDS by Charles Koburger [297], an American Coast Guard officer, detailed the make-up of the British forces used in the operations and noted that, for the first time, "computer faced computer" in warfare. This replaced the old "gunboat diplomacy" of the nineteenth century.

A retired admiral, Peter Stanford [469], lamented that even though the Royal Navy had once again proven its worth, this time in the Persian Gulf crisis of the late 1980s, promises of restoration of losses and new construction were not being fulfilled.

TABLE OF PARTICIPATING FORCES: MILITARY, NAVAL, AIR, AND OTHER

Note: A. = Argentine; B. = British.

Personnel:

A. Estimates vary, c. 13,000, mostly conscripts, ashore on the Falklands/Malvinas, mostly in the Port Stanley area.

B. 19,000 in the Task Force, voluntary, mostly naval personnel, plus 9,000 more in merchant ships.

Armies:

A. Various conscripts and commando units.

B. Amphibious forces: counting marines, 3rd Commando Brigade (40, 42, 45 Commando), 2nd and 3rd Parachute Battalions, Special Air Service (SAS), Special Boat Service (SBS).

Navies:

A.   31,000 total for the navy (including 12,000 conscripts), 6000 marines.

B.   19,000 in the task force.

Air Forces:

A.   Huertas [257] claimed Argentina used about 300 aircraft and lost about 100; flew 505 combat sorties of which 272 reached targets; 452 transport aircraft landings at Port Stanley; 4 Super Etendard aircraft and 5 EXOCET missiles sank 2 British ships; 133 sorties of A-4B Skyhawks using free-fall bombs sank 3 British ships; 796 army helicopter missions; Koburger [297] claimed 230 aircraft and helicopters, 140 being high-performance jet aircraft; JANE'S [267] incorrectly claimed 16 Super Etendard and 14 A-4Q attack aircraft for the Argentine navy; Middlebrook [341] said there were 50 aircraft of the air force and navy available for supplying the islands.

B.   83 Harrier VSTOL jet attack aircraft and various types of helicopters.

Warships:

A.   54 ships of all classes, including 1 aircraft carrier, 1 cruiser, 8 destroyers, and 4 submarines. The Argentine fleet withdrew completely to home bases after the sinking of BELGRANO on 2 May and never operated again during the campaign.

B.   In the task force, 44 warships, 22 auxiliary ships, and 50 STUFT involved; JANE'S [268], 1982–1983, noted INVINCIBLE was to be sold to Australia; an ex-fleet tanker was begged back from Chile; Koburger [297] claimed a total of 116 ships.

Weapons:

A.   EXOCET missiles; 14 EXOCET and aerial bomb warheads hit British naval targets but failed to explode, primarily because the fuzzes had insufficient time to activate.

B.   Sidewinder air-to-air missiles were very successful; Sea Harriers scored 24 hits with 27 Sidewinder air-to-air missiles fired.

Civilian Ships:

A. Few, if any, were used.

B. Ships-Taken-Up-for-Trade (STUFT) = over 50 merchant ships and 9,000 merchant ship personnel.

Losses:

A. ships = BELGRANO, a submarine, and several auxiliaries.

B. ships = 4 destroyers (SHEFFIELD, 10 May, ARDENT, 22 May, ANTELOPE, 24 May, and COVENTRY, 25 May, and 2 important logistics landing ships, SIR GALAHAD and SIR TRISTRAM, 8 June); many others damaged.

A. aircraft = various estimates: 103 plus 14 probables; 105; 109 from Max Hastings [228, 229]; 75 aircraft and 25 helicopters from Middlebrook [341]; about 40% of the strength of the air force; 31 of these were brought down by Harriers; 45 pilots were lost not including helicopter pilots.

B. aircraft = 34; 9 Harriers and 25 helicopters; 4 pilots not including helicopter pilots.

A. killed = 652 (announced number, 323 from BELGRANO).

B. killed = 255.

A. wounded = over 1000.

B. wounded = 777

A. POWs = 79, the British marine contingents at Falkland/Malvinas and South Georgia islands.

B. POWs = 12,700 Argentines (some small variations in estimates).

Chapter 7

OPERATIONS

NARRATIVE ACCOUNTS OF THE CAMPAIGN

The Falklands/Malvinas campaign has been put forward as the classic case of a limited war: limited in weaponry, geography, time, tactics, and strategy. On the subject of limited warfare see the works of Morton Halperin [219, 220].

A Pakistani Army general, E. H. Dar [119], analyzed the strategy of the war. He concluded that the Argentine leadership was ill-prepared and obstinate: the British were left with only one option, counter-invasion. Richard Lebow in the JOURNAL OF STRATEGIC STUDIES [315] concluded that there were serious miscalculations on both sides, "two serious and mutually reinforcing misjudgments" (p. 5); specifically, "a penny pinching mentality" of the Thatcher government and self-deception by the Argentine Junta, who became prisoners of their own policy.

U.S. admiral Harry Train [491] analyzed the campaign for the Naval War College. It was the first to use modern cruise missiles against warships and the first to use nuclear-powered attack submarines. He presented details on the factors influencing selection of the landing site. He noted that the 14 unexploded Argentine bombs could have doubled the actual British losses.

Osprey Publishing formulated a trilogy, the MEN-AT-ARMS series [391], which included British and Argentine forces: I. William Fowler [164] for land forces, II. Adrian English and Anthony Watts [140] for naval forces, and III. Ray Braybrook [59] for air forces. These covered operations only, and not all of them, e.g., nothing on submarine activities. E. F. Gueritz [211] wrote an article praising the cooperativeness of the services in this joint British operation.

Air marshal M. J. Armitage [12] described details of the opposing forces. The Argentines built up their total forces to 12,300 men. There were 31 airfields scattered throughout the islands; 5 of them were all-weather strips. At Stanley the main airfield was 4100 feet long with one taxiing strip and one maintenance hangar. The Stanley field was bombed several times but was quickly repaired and used by the Argentines during most of the war.

Derek Wood and Mark Hewish [530] wrote a series of articles on the campaign, e.g., the air war, missile operations, and naval operations, in INTERNATIONAL DEFENCE REVIEW. Robert Reginald and Jeffrey Elliot [427] characterized the campaign as a "tempest in a teapot," and persisted in using that analogy: "tea party," "simmering brew," "the pot boils over," and "to the last dregs," with several errors included, e.g., BELGRANO sunk with Tigerfish Mark 24 torpedoes and "melting the aluminum superstructure" of SHEFFIELD.

General accounts and assessments of the campaign included: Peter Way [518]; Norma Stewart [470]; Jurg Meister [335] in German; Stewart Menaul [337]; Ruben Moro [366, 367]; Julian Lider [319]; R. Planchar [403] in French; Derek Oakley [388]; Elizabeth Young [534]; Jeffrey Record [424]; and John Laffin in BRASSEY'S BATTLES: 3500 YEARS OF CONFLICT, CAMPAIGNS, AND WARS FROM A TO Z [305, pp. 163–65], devoting three pages to the Falklands/Malvinas campaign.

Seven publications by Paul Beaver of the Jane's organization elaborated on various aspects of the British military and naval forces involved: helicopters [30], the aircraft carrier in general [31] and HMS INVINCIBLE [33] in particular, the Royal Marines [35], a military encyclopedia [32], naval air power [541], and a survey

of the Royal Navy [34]. In 1945 Great Britain had 52 aircraft
carriers with 18 under construction. None of that "attack" class
of carriers existed in the 1980s. The Royal Navy introduced most
of the modern innovations for aircraft carriers: the angled deck,
the mirrored landing system, the armored flight deck, the steam
catapult, and, for the two which did participate in the Falklands
task force, the VSTOL Harrier, and the ski-jump flight deck.

British air warfare, aircraft carriers, and aircraft have been
other topics of interest: Norman Friedman in BRITISH CARRIER
AVIATION [176] stressed the long list of British innovations in
carrier operations; Peter Garrison in "CV": CARRIER AVIA-
TION [190]; Richard Humble in AIRCRAFT CARRIERS [258],
which once again denounced the government for abandoning
naval aviation; Ray Sturtivant, BRITISH NAVAL AVIATION:
THE FLEET AIR ARM, 1917–1990 [475]; Ray Williams, ROYAL
NAVY AIRCRAFT SINCE 1945 [527], which covered 44 aircraft
types; John Winton, AIR POWER AT SEA: 1945 TO TODAY
[529]; Leo Marriott in ROYAL NAVY AIRCRAFT CARRIERS,
1945–1990 [330]; and Edwin Hoyt in CARRIER WARS: NAVAL
AVIATION FROM WORLD WAR 2 TO THE PERSIAN GULF
[255], which incorporated coverage of the Falklands campaign.
The "howler" in Hoyt was that the Argentine aircraft carrier had
launched the air attack which sank HMS ARDENT and was "the
greatest shock of the sea war in the Falklands" (pp. 251-52). The
Argentine fleet conducted no operations after 2 May; ARDENT
was sunk on 21 May. No doubt a better case can be made that the
attack on SHEFFIELD on 4 May was a greater shock than that on
ARDENT.

Air defense of the task force and of the landings turned out to
be the most formidable problem for the British. During the 1950s,
1960s, and 1970s the Royal Navy maintained "attack" aircraft
carriers such as ARK ROYAL. These carriers had complements
of airborne early warning (AEW) aircraft which provided long-
range radar surveillance. The last one was deactivated in 1978.
The INVINCIBLE and HERMES were much smaller and had no
room for AEW aircraft. So the task force had to make do with
an inferior set-up based on the use of radar picket ships, usually
variations of destroyers and frigates, stationed out from the task
force in the direction from which an air attack might come. This

arrangement rendered the picket destroyers vulnerable to air attack, but protection for the "High Value Units" (HVUs) such as the carriers and large transports was maintained. In the end, it was the destroyer-types which "paid the price"—four were sunk and several more were damaged—and no HVUs were hit. Tony Dyson [135], naval commander, formulated a "pictorial history" of HERMES, 1959–1984. There were over 150 illustrations. Construction on HERMES commenced in 1944; the BELGRANO was only about five years older.

John Coote entitled his article which reviewed the campaign "Send Her Victorious" [105], an allusion to the name of one of the attack aircraft carriers scrapped earlier by the Royal Navy. David Smith and Andrew Wynn [458] published a pictorial on HMS ARK ROYAL, another small carrier which was completed after the campaign was over. The authorities must have regretted not having these useful warships available at the time of the campaign in 1982.

Two works focused on both air forces. AIR WAR SOUTH ATLANTIC by Jeffrey Ethell and Alfred Price [144] detailed preparation and operations of the air forces. R. A. Mason [334] reflected on the air war.

Others concentrated on the Argentine air forces. Salvador Mafe Huertas, ARGENTINE AIR FORCES IN THE FALKLANDS CONFLICT [257] provided details and illustrations on their extensive and sometimes spectacular operations. Robert Nutwell [387] assessed Argentine air operations against the British fleet. The successes were spectacular and would have been more so if bomb and EXOCET fuzzes had activated. But the price was high, about 75 attack aircraft, about half by surface-to-air missiles and about half by Harriers. Alberto Philippi [400] was an Argentine Skyhawk pilot, originally aboard the aircraft carrier, but operating later from land bases. He was shot down by a Harrier during an attack on naval ships, parachuted into the sea, came ashore, and was rescued by a ranch manager.

If the air force was the most successful and praised force for the Argentines, the Harrier aircraft and their pilots were the most widely acclaimed forces of the British. John Godden [197] edited a full account about these fascinating "jump-jets," i.e., they were VSTOL and normally took off using the "ski-jump" facility at the bow of the carrier. Twenty-eight Sea Harriers (i.e., Royal Navy [RN]) and 14 GR3s (Royal Air Force [RAF]) participated in the campaign; 9 were lost, including 4 pilots. Godden described them as "dauntingly outnumbered" but achieving a "legendary reputation." Recall that Brian Hanrahan [222] described a Harrier attack and symbolized the concern, reputation, and media difficulties with the famous phrase with which he entitled his book on the Falklands, "I COUNTED THEM ALL OUT AND I COUNTED THEM ALL BACK." In fact there were 8 Harriers on that attack wave.

Other accounts of Harriers were by Francis Mason [333], B. Myles [374], and Alfred Price [415], who presented the most detail on Harriers and the Falklands/Malvinas campaign: they flew 300 sorties; they carried the Sidewinder infra-red homing missile for air-to-air action and almost immediately gained superiority in the sky; and there were no air-to-air Harrier losses.

Harriers enjoyed spectacular acclaim; helicopters were also successful, vital, and much praised for providing less glamorous "work-horse" functions. RUSI JOURNAL published a special supplement [441] on the military helicopter. J. M. Milne [347], Michael Gething [195], Bill Gunston [214], and John Hamilton [221] presented general and illustrated accounts of their operations.

AVIATION WEEK AND SPACE TECHNOLOGY [16, 429] devoted extensive coverage to the campaign, particularly the "hi-tech" weapons, electronics, and countermeasures. The French, notably, were anxious to publicize actions in which French-designed weaponry had been used: e.g., EXOCETs, Mirage fighters, and Roland surface-to-air missiles. The French company building Roland missiles accused the British of lying about Harrier losses due to their missiles. French Roland claimed eight missiles had been fired at the British; five hit Harriers, one hit a bomb (!), and two could not be accounted for.

Submarines were utilized extensively by both sides but their operations have been least publicized. British nuclear-powered submarines effectively drove the Argentine navy from the high seas. The well-informed John Moore and Richard Compton-Hall [357] reviewed modern submarine warfare. Scheina [449] wrote on the Argentine submarine operations. Juan Murguizur [371] looked to the future in appraising Argentine submarine potential. Lessons from the campaign caused reevaluation of the structure of the Argentine fleet. The determination was that more and more modern submarines would be necessary. A plan for obtaining six submarines of German design, two to be built in Germany and four in Argentina, has been implemented. In the revised edition of the history of the torpedo (1991), Edwyn Gray [548] incorporated coverage of torpedo use in this campaign.

Bryan Perrett reviewed WEAPONS OF THE FALKLANDS CONFLICT [399]. Individual weapons and systems used by both sides in the campaign have been described. THE FALKLANDS ARMOURY, edited by Mark Dartford [121], presented illustrations and schematics of the weapons and equipment of the conflict. Informative, authoritative, and detailed was Antony Preston, SEA COMBAT OFF THE FALKLANDS [413]. He noted that there was a serious gap of air early warning, that the ski-jump nose ramp meant Harriers could take off with more weight (fuel and ammunition) but that conventional aircraft could not use those carriers, and that reports of aluminum superstructures on British ships burning and melting were unfounded.

The weapon receiving most attention and most interest was EXOCET, a powerful surface-to-surface and air-to-surface missile which can be, and was in the campaign, launched from ships, aircraft, and land. It was a "sea skimmer" which contained a 360-pound warhead. Antony Preston [411] and B. Estival and J. Guillot [143] wrote of its development and use. It was designed by the French in the late 1960s and by 1977, 17 nations had ordered 1000.

Alfred Price, INSTRUMENTS OF DARKNESS: THE HISTORY OF ELECTRONIC WARFARE [416], presented the early history of technological advances in warfare. ELECTRONIC WARFARE was reviewed by Mario DeArcangelis [124], covering developments from about 1900 through the mid-1980s. David Kiely [288, 289] wrote general accounts of both surface weapons and naval electronic warfare. Alastair Mitchell [353] reviewed the history and development of radar in a series of articles in the journal WARSHIP.

There has been a plethora of histories of specialized forces of the British, e.g., SAS and SBS, but information about detailed operations, specific achievements, and individual exploits has been slow in coming. Such publication theoretically violated secrecy limitations. Even John Gardner [189] in the fictionalized James Bond thriller was vague in recounting exactly what "007" did in secret operations during the campaign. William Seymour [451] and Nigel Foster [160] wrote general histories of British special forces. James Ladd [302, 304], Philip Warner [516], and Peter Davis [122] wrote of SBS and Royal Marine commandos. Tony Geraghty, WHO DARES WINS: INSIDE THE SPECIAL AIR SERVICE [194], has a chapter on the South Atlantic campaign.

INTELLIGENCE OPERATIONS

As in the case of submarine operations, many questions remained about details of intelligence operations during the campaign. What did leaders of each side know and when did they know it? Why was British intelligence such a spectacular failure in the matters of the South Georgia incident and the invasion? In exactly what forms and to what extent did American intelligence assist the British? If that was extensive, why was the much-touted American intelligence such a failure as well? Why the imbroglio around the circumstances of the sinking of the BELGRANO? Did the Russians provide intelligence information to the Argentines? What contributions did other potential allies make, e.g., France and Chile; for Great Britain, Peru, Israel, and Libya for Argentina? Speculative assertions have been forthcoming providing answers to some of these questions. Presumably the 30–Year Rule will apply and it will be at least that time until more is known.

Intelligence capabilities or lack of them have been noted. Guillermo Makin [326] reviewed the preliminaries and pointed to the failure of British intelligence in anticipating the Argentine invasion.

Recall that JANE'S [268] and similar annual published compilations [e.g., 101, 104, 376] were among the first sources researched by intelligence and other analysts. An extraordinary increase in the use of public libraries in Portsmouth and Plymouth reportedly was experienced. The prominent strategic historian, Lawrence Freedman, wrote on this in INTELLIGENCE AND NATIONAL

SECURITY [174], a relatively new journal. It was limited war "par excellence," confined in space, time, and participation. Freedman evaluated British intelligence. He stressed two controversies: the failure to anticipate the Argentine invasion, and the BELGRANO affair, which has been investigated by the House of Commons Foreign Affairs Committee of 1984–1985 Session [252]. British intelligence for all of Latin America was "massively overworked," the attaches being forced to concentrate on selling arms and thus neglecting intelligence obligations. ENDURANCE and U.S. intelligence monitored much traffic after the invasion but U.S. intelligence provided no warning of imminent invasion. The best information was from SIGINT, signals intelligence. In summary, the British overestimated the number of Argentine aircraft available (247 when there were only 130) but underestimated the quality and training of pilots. The French provided information on specific airplanes and the EXOCETs. Chile facilitated SAS and reconnaissance operations around Argentine bases.

David King [290] reacted to Freedman's article in INTELLIGENCE AND NATIONAL SECURITY [174]. To him, it was now clear that perfect intelligence would not have prevented the invasion. The Argentine equivalent to the FRANKS REPORT [168], the RATTENBACH REPORT [422], divulged that all planning was secret and that the original timetable was accelerated by several months.

Jeffrey Richelson and Desmond Ball [430] were enlightening on specific intelligence procedures; an intelligence "club," the United States, Britain, Canada, Australia, and New Zealand, during World War II and after, formulated cooperative efforts that had continued subsequently.

"Britain's Pearl Harbor" was the title used by Simon Jenkins [271] to denounce British authorities and American intelligence for failure to anticipate the Argentine invasion which, he claimed, was obviously well-planned long in advance. He disputed the FRANKS REPORT [168], which stated the invasion was so sudden it could not have been foreseen. Whitehall was obsessed to the point of fanaticism, cutting resources without regard to difficult decisions. Gerald Hopple [245] also used Pearl Harbor, among other surprise attacks, to compare with the Argentine invasion.

Middlebrook [341] claimed the Russians closely monitored events in the South Atlantic but gave no assistance to Argentina. Apparently the Argentines asked the Russians for assistance, including intelligence information. The Russians agreed but, in practice, it was impossible to find compatible communication links to access the information.

Information about intelligence operations during the campaign, i.e., tactical intelligence, can be found in David Ridlon, "Shots in the Dark: British Tactical Intelligence in the Falklands War" [431]. Ridlon, an American army intelligence officer, described such operations as extensive patrolling by small units of special forces put ashore by boat or helicopter, in some cases weeks before the actual landings. At least one SAS team operated on the Argentine mainland. There was also "the Phantom Voice," Falkland resident Reginald Silvey, an amateur radio operator who disrupted and confused Argentine communications.

ARGENTINE OPERATIONS

"Operacion Rosario" was the official name of the plan for the invasion of the Falklands/Malvinas Islands by the Argentines. EL RESCATE DE LAS MALVINAS by Martin Berger [48] presented the historical background and Haroldo Foulkes [162] reviewed the "74 dias." Carlos Busser [68] surveyed all pertinent events from the diplomacy of the mid–1960s through the surrender and aftermath. He began by quoting George Bernard Shaw and incorporated the alleged Argentine attack on the British carrier INVINCIBLE. Oscar Jofre [272] described Argentine defense operations and Daniel Terzano [479] focused on "Puerto Argentino," Port Stanley.

The origins of the incident which became the pretext for the invasion by Argentina can be traced to a business undertaking by a scrap dealer in Buenos Aires, S. C. Davidoff. In 1978 Davidoff obtained a contract with Christian Salvesen Company of Leith, Edinburgh, Scotland, to dismantle several obsolete whaling facilities on the island of South Georgia, 700 miles southeast of the Falklands/Malvinas. South Georgia was a dependency of the Falklands/Malvinas. In the process of executing that contract in mid-March 1982 Davidoff involved units of the Argentine navy, a procedure with some precedents. However, in this case, the Argentine naval authorities, apparently acting on their own initiative, decided to provoke an incident and take over South Georgia. On 19 March the Argentine flag was raised on South Georgia at Leith harbor. ENDURANCE was ordered in. The Argentines sent warships. On 26 March the Junta decided to invade the Falklands/Malvinas. The Argentine navy conducted most of the operations of the invasion of the Falklands/Malvinas, then army forces were brought in in large numbers.

Operations of Argentine commandos were chronicled by Isidoro Ruiz Moreno [361]. The 601 and 602 Companies conducted intelligence and watched the Kelpers. He presented the Argentine version of a controversial incident, the death of Colonel Herbert Jones, commander of a parachute regiment at the battle of Goose Green on 29 May. Jones was shot, the British version contended, while receiving the surrender of some Argentine soldiers. He was awarded the Victoria Cross. Moreno said Lt. Juan Gomez shot Jones while he was trying to trick some soldiers into surrendering. This incident was investigated by several journalists (Hastings [229], Bishop and Witherow [52], Fox [166], and the historian Middlebrook [342]). Jones bled to death.

The life and conditions of the Argentine conscripts and others on the front line have been best depicted by a freelance journalist, Daniel Kon [298, 300]. His LOS CHICOS DE LA GUERRA was a bestseller, was turned into a feature film [299], and was translated into English [300]. Eight long interviews were summarized. Conditions depicted were hunger, frustration, boredom, trauma, and neglect. Clearly, authorities at the highest (i.e., the Junta) and lowest (i.e., officers and non-commissioned officers [NCOs]) levels did or cared little for the conscripts. Kon indicted the incompetence, heartlessness, and overly patriotic rhetoric of those authorities.

Controversy has arisen about Argentine air operations, especially a large number of seemingly confident claims of severe damage inflicted on the HVUs (High Value Units) of the British task force. Jesus Romero Briasco and Salvador Mafe Huertas [435] presented FALKLANDS, WITNESS OF BATTLES, a review of the air war with many pictures. Jorge Luis Colombo [100], a commander in the Argentine naval air force, recounted sorties of the Super Etendard fast jet attack aircraft in PROCEEDINGS OF THE NAVAL INSTITUTE. Super Etendards were the most sophisticated aircraft operated by Argentina. The French had delivered the aircraft and several EXOCET missiles shortly before the war began. More were expected soon. Then the French suddenly withdrew, leaving the Argentines to complete training, install the missiles, and conduct operations on their own. He then described some specific attacks, e.g., the sinking of the ATLANTIC CONVEYOR on 25 May and the successful attack against INVINCIBLE on 30 May. The latter, Colombo claimed, involved six aircraft. They surprised the carrier and positively observed smoke from the damage inflicted as they departed the area. In a book Pablo Carballo [81] reviewed a number of first-hand operations of Argentine pilots supplemented by colorful, realistic pictures of jet attacks, for example on the frigate ARGONAUT and on INVINCIBLE, depicted as exploding and smoking from several places below decks. Jeffrey Ethell [143] was also enlightening on the Super Etendard situation. The French had delivered five; the Argentines used one for parts and operated with four. The initiatives demonstrated by the Argentine pilots and support staff were extraordinary. They wrote their own operations routine and installed the EXOCET missiles without expert assistance. Argentine failures were also reviewed: technical defects and bomb-fusing problems. Many Argentine weapons were manufactured in Great Britain!

Argentine air force commodore Ruben Moro [366, 367], a C-130 transport pilot, surveyed the history of the conflict. He accused the British of systematically hiding and disguising their own losses while exaggerating Argentine casualties, e.g., damages inflicted on the British aircraft carriers and losses of Harriers. Moro also placed maximum blame for the conflict at the feet of the United States.

Damage inflicted on the British task force was extensive, according to Argentine authorities. These claims were presented with obvious confidence and there were published pictures, actually drawings, in Argentine newspapers and magazines depicting a burning and sinking INVINCIBLE. Juan Murguizur [372] presented the Argentine view on battle losses, concluding that 38 British ships were heavily damaged, including two aircraft carriers, e.g., HERMES on 4 May, the day SHEFFIELD was sunk. Other Argentine air attacks were claimed to have damaged the liners CANBERRA and UGANDA and the flagship, HERMES. Peter Beck [36, p. 6] noted this and recalled a satire in a Chilean newspaper:

Question: What news from Buenos Aires?
Answer: The British sent three planes to the Falklands. The Argentines shot down seven of them!

The bi-monthly Argentine journal AEROESPACIO/AEROSPACE (March-April 1983, pp. 19–32) [4] included an account of an inspection conducted by Argentine authorities of HMS INVIN-CIBLE after her return to the Portsmouth naval base. The investigators noted an area "suspiciously recently painted."

Middlebrook [341, p. 202] elaborated on this dispute. "The most controversial air action," the INVINCIBLE attack, occurred on 30 May. The last Argentine EXOCET was used along with bombs, but the target was AVENGER—INVINCIBLE was 30 miles away. All of the projectiles missed. Three post-war Argentine accounts continued to insist on the INVINCIBLE story.

BRITISH OPERATIONS

"Operation Corporate" was the name given to the campaign by the British. The actual battle phase lasted 74 days. The Argentines occupied the Falkland/Malvinas Islands on 2 April, South Georgia was recaptured by the British on 25 April, the British commenced active operations at recovery on 1 May, and Port Stanley was officially regained and the Argentines surrendered on 14 June.

The hastily assembled British task force sailed in two group-ings, on 3–5 April and 6–7 April, proceeding to Ascension Island, about halfway to the Falklands/Malvinas, where necessary reloading and rearranging for combat amphibious operations were concluded.

The best single source of British operations during the campaign was a semi-official survey by the head of the Naval History Branch, David Brown, THE ROYAL NAVY AND THE

FALKLANDS WAR [61]. The writing, research, illustrations, maps, and index were all superb but there was no analysis. Detailed descriptions of the background, British operations at sea, in the air, and on land, and the aftermath were included. There was nothing on submarine operations, which remained secret, and little on the BELGRANO incident.

Roger Perkins, OPERATION PARAQUAT: THE BATTLE OF SOUTH GEORGIA [396, p. vii], recounted the scrap metal imbroglio and "the least known and least understood episode in the Anglo-Argentine conflict." Two of Britain's most secret military organizations were highlighted, the Army's Special Air Service Regiment and the Royal Marine's Special Boat Service. Twenty-two SAS men were killed in a helicopter accident.

One of the first overt acts by the British was the bombing of the Stanley airfield on 1 May, reportedly the date of the beginning of aggressive operations of the campaign. That bombing was by a long-range Vulcan bomber from Ascension Island, which flew 6800 miles round trip, the longest flight ever made by bomber aircraft in the history of air warfare. Eleven refuelling tankers were required for the flight. A total of five Vulcan bomber raids from Ascension were completed, dropping 1000-pound bombs, mostly on or near Stanley airfield. Six failed to explode.

Several works focused on the naval war and on individual classes of ships: C. J. Meyer on the LEANDER CLASS [340], a frigate; Leo Marriott, TYPE 42 [332], a destroyer class of which there were a total of 14, including SHEFFIELD and COVENTRY which were lost; Leo Marriott, ROYAL NAVY FRIGATES, 1945–1983 [331]; C. H. Layman [314], commanding officer of ARGONAUT, a LEANDER class frigate which was seriously damaged; and Brenda Lewis, "The Loss of HMS COVENTRY" [318], sunk while operating on the air defense screen. Kenneth Harmon [223] provided some technical details about deficiencies associated with the loss of SHEFFIELD.

The British air war was recounted by Rodney Burden [65]. Cindy Buxton, a journalist, wrote SURVIVAL—SOUTH ATLANTIC [70], coining the term "Red Iceberg," which described ENDURANCE.

The British writers on the land phases of the campaign continually and consistently stressed the high levels of professionalism, dedication, morale, and initiative of the Commandos. The amphibious phase of the British operations was placed in perspective by John Jackson, FROM INCHON TO SAN CARLOS [266]. Brigadier Julian Thompson, Royal Marines, recounted his experiences as commander of 3 Commando Brigade in NO PICNIC [480]. High points included South Georgia, the initial landings on the Falklands, Goose Green, the "yomp" east, and Port Stanley. "Yomp" was the term for travelling overland. MARCH TO THE SOUTH ATLANTIC: 42 COMMANDO IN THE FALKLANDS [508] and TAKE THAT HILL!: THE ROYAL MARINES IN THE FALKLANDS WAR [509] were by Nick Vaux, commanding officer of 42 Commando. 2 PARA FALKLANDS: THE BATTALION AT WAR [178] was John Frost's story of that special unit "from Aldershot to Port Stanley via San Carlos, Goose Green, Bluff Cove, and Wireless Ridge," the names of most of the major land operations of the war. Hugh McManners [325], captain of Royal Artillery, touted his "worm's eye view" as a Falklands/Malvinas commando.

Even the least glamorous task has been chronicled: Rick Jolly, THE RED AND GREEN LIFE MACHINE: A DIARY OF THE FALKLANDS FIELD HOSPITAL [276]. Jolly detailed the activities of this navy-marine hospital unit.

Interest in the campaign was wide ranging. Writers from Soviet Russia completed a number of articles on logistics, electronic warfare, and naval operations in various military and naval journals, as described by Ralph Bruner [63].

THE "BELGRANO" AND THE "PONTING"
AFFAIRS

Alleged scandals erupted in Great Britain over incidents during the campaign, so serious as to be compared with the Watergate scandal in the United States. They have continued long after the successful completion and the glorious return home of the participants. Two affairs, themselves related, persisted well into the late 1980s. BELGRANO was the Argentine cruiser torpedoed by a British nuclear-attack submarine and Ponting was the name of a government bureaucrat who was put on trial for violation of the Official Secrets Act.

After 1 May, apparently, all parties accepted the fact of overt warfare. On that date two Argentine naval task forces were operating at sea west of the Falkland/Malvinas Islands, one led by the aircraft carrier to the north and one led by the cruiser to the south. On 2 May HMS CONQUEROR, a nuclear-powered attack submarine, which had been tracking the southern group consisting of the pre–World War II–built cruiser (ex-USS PHOE-NIX) GENERAL BELGRANO and two destroyers for two days, fired three Mark 8, World War II–type torpedoes at BELGRANO. Two hit, one knocking off the bow—for the third time!—and the other striking berthing-messing areas, killing many below-decks. The third hit one of the destroyers but it failed to explode. BELGRANO sank in 40 minutes. The destroyers immediately departed as they were instructed to do. The death toll was 321 or 323 of the 1093 men aboard BELGRANO. For months the figure was quoted as 368, an incorrect total. Middlebrook [341] has studied this incident thoroughly.

The sinking of the Argentine cruiser BELGRANO, one of the two major warships in the Argentine fleet, precipitated a sensational reaction in Great Britain. Many questions were raised about when, where, and why this attack and sinking took place. In this affair, a number of issues have been raised, some of them having to do with international agreements on the conduct of combat operations during limited wars. The Falklands/Malvinas campaign was the consummate limited war, rigidly controlled by international law using such techniques as Exclusion Zones, Rules of Engagement, certain restraints on weaponry, and restricted areas.

Christopher Craig [110] wrote a professional assessment of Rules of Engagement, a process utilizing accepted practices of international law. The British declared various degrees of Exclusion Zones beginning on 7 April. These were promulgated to the international community including informing the Argentines of such zones and changes in degree of the rules. These matters were emotive issues in the sinking of BELGRANO. All agreed she was outside of a previously declared Exclusion Zone and headed away from the Falklands at the time she was torpedoed. Middlebrook [341] presented some extenuating circumstances. The British wanted to attack the aircraft carrier but there was no contact at the time. BELGRANO was outside the Exclusion Zone and headed west, but not en route to home. The Argentine authorities had been informed that any warship which was deemed to be threatening after the beginning of operations on 1 May was subject to attack. There were also delays and temporary disruptions of communication with CONQUEROR.

The British first declared a 200–mile Exclusion Zone around the Falkland/Malvinas Islands, and then expanded it to a Total Exclusion Zone. G. M. Dillon [129] included a lengthy explanation of events around the BELGRANO sinking. John Laffin wrote "The Truth about the BELGRANO" for SPECTATOR [307]. In an intelligence assessment, Lawrence Freedman [174] explained that SIGINT was picking up conflicting information, some that the southern force planned to attack, some ordering it to break off, and definite orders for the northern group with the aircraft carrier to attack. Apparently the Argentine aircraft carrier prepared to launch an air attack against the task force on 1 May but the wind was insufficient for carrier operations. There were some delays in British SIGINT decoding.

The Clive Ponting affair extended the controversy into the late 1980s. In July 1984 this bureaucrat within the Ministry of Defence leaked documents related to BELGRANO to Tam Dalyell, a Labour MP. Ponting insisted his responsibility was to Parliament, not the government. He was prosecuted under the Official Secrets Act of 1911. In the meantime the log of CONQUEROR and the diary of Narendra Sethia, a crewman, disappeared, and government agents searching for intelligence information were involved in the death of Hilda Murrell, an aunt of an official. The Ponting trial lasted two weeks and ended with his acquittal. Lowell Gustafson [215] recounted these bizarre events.

Ponting himself has not remained reticent. RIGHT TO KNOW: THE INSIDE STORY OF THE "BELGRANO" AFFAIR [406] and SECRECY IN BRITAIN [407] were two publications. Ponting attended the University of Reading and went into government service, at the Ministry of Defence, in 1970 and resigned in 1984, at which time he was arrested and tried at Old Bailey for violation of the secrets act. He recalled his disenchantment, especially with what he saw as excessive spending in the Ministry of Defence. While still at the Ministry he wrote a summary of events, "the

Battle for the Truth," dubbed "the Crown Jewels." Ponting [406, pp. 3–12] said he was most concerned about an alleged cover-up and government misstatements. Richard Norton-Taylor [385] reviewed the Ponting Affair, noting these events were insightful about the culture and intrigue of Whitehall. He and others saw the trial as a purely political one and the acquittal as a humiliating defeat for the government and a blow, perhaps fatal, at the official secrets process.

Questions, accusations, recriminations, and sensation have continued over this series of events for several years in Great Britain. The Foreign Affairs Committee of the House of Commons (Session of 1984–1985) investigated "Events of the Weekend of 1st and 2nd May 1982" [252]. What became known as the "Tam Dalyell line," accusations of government conspiracy and Thatcher's fanaticism to crush Argentina, was most comprehensively incorporated in THE SINKING OF THE "BELGRANO" [191, 192] by Arthur Gavshon, a journalist, and Desmond Rice, a business executive and novelist (under the name Desmond Meiring). They emphasized allegations such as the location of BELGRANO outside the Exclusion Zone, heading in the direction of home, and creating this incident to quash the Peruvian peace plan. Criticisms abound against this book, e.g., those of Max Hastings [229] and Lawrence Freedman [173].

Duncan Campbell has an article in the NEW STATESMAN, "The BELGRANO Cover-up" [80]. He accused the government of deceiving Parliament and compared the scandal to the Watergate affair of the United States. Paul Foot [158], also in NEW STATESMAN, "How the Peace Was Torpedoed," accused the government of sinking BELGRANO to "scupper" a peace settlement. The FRANKS REPORT [168] focused only on the period up to the invasion. Thus, the BELGRANO affair was not reviewed, Foot noted. See the versions of Tam Dalyell [115, 116, 117] which are presented elsewhere (p. 23).

Reminiscent of the Nuremberg Trials of the mid–1940s, several interested persons, calling themselves the Belgrano Action Group, conducted a formal, judicial-type enquiry 7–8 November 1986 and published their findings in 1988 [45]. Clive Ponting wrote the introduction. The trial was held in the Hampstead Town Hall. There were accusations of government cover-up, loss of official documents such as diplomatic telegrams and the log of HMS CONQUEROR, a naval initiative to end cut-backs, and a device to quash important peace efforts.

"Sink the BELGRANO!" by Steven Berkoff [49] was a play performed at the Halfmoon and Mermaid theaters in September and October of 1986. It included an opening statement, "the still small voice of truth," by Tam Dalyell and characters such as "Maggot Scratcher," "Pimp," and "Nit," and was obviously not sympathetic to the government. Berkoff explained that he was inspired by the book of Arthur Gavshon and Desmond Rice [192].

Another incident in the aftermath of the BELGRANO affair involved Diana Gould, a housewife from Cirencester who openly questioned Thatcher about BELGRANO. She published her story [203] and was called "a prodigious West Country battle-axe" and "Tam Dalyell in drag."

LOGISTICS

The Argentines were relatively close to the islands, and, especially during the month of April before active belligerence began, they were able to fly and ship in huge amounts of equipment, materiel, and supplies and large numbers of personnel. After the British task force arrived in the area, the Argentines were unable to provide any secure and reliable supply by sea. They were able to maintain air supply activities throughout the campaign, usually confined to the night air operations of transports from the mainland to the airfield at Stanley.

Under the circumstances of the post–World War II draw-down, preparation and logistics for this campaign presented the British with seemingly insurmountable challenges. A series of major reductions of forces, for example in 1957 and 1981, had been announced, and indeed, the most recent one was actually in progress early in 1982. Those dispositions were altered. One aircraft carrier was diverted from its intended turnover to Australia and a vital fleet oil tanker was recalled after having been installed in the Chilean navy. Even if aircraft carriers could somehow be expropriated, the versions capable of supporting extended air operations away from bases and defense had long been eliminated. Much of the active fleet which was left was committed to NATO. There were insufficient numbers of support ships. There were no advanced bases. The logistical situation for the British appeared impossible. The Falklands/Malvinas were 8000 miles from Great Britain and there were no nearby bases available for British use. David Brown [61] covered this feature well. Against all of these odds, superhuman efforts were exerted and a large task force was gathered together and the necessary forces of all types were mobilized to be forwarded to the vicinity of the islands.

An impressive logistical expedient employed by the British, obviously with extensive prior planning and anticipation, was "Ships-Taken-Up-From-Trade" (STUFT). The Department of Trade chartered—terms such as "Shanghaied" and "impressed" have been used—54 ships from 33 commercial companies. These were immediately modified for combat (guns, protection, helicopter platforms, communications facilities, etc.), and sent off in convoy to the South Atlantic.

STUFT filled many logistical gaps. The definitive account was that of Roger Villar [510, 511], a captain of the Royal Navy. All types of ships were commandeered: luxury liners such as QE2 and CANBERRA (a helicopter pad was installed over the center swimming pool), huge car ferries, tugs, fishing trawlers (mine sweepers), and a hospital ship. W. J. Tustin [498] presented an overview of the logistics situation in two parts. Richard Humble [259, p. 225] described the operation as "massive press-gang raids" to obtain a fleet train and "a magnificent national effort." Portsmouth naval base performed most of the modifications and conversions.

BRITISH SUPERLINERS OF THE SIXTIES by Philip Dawson [123], published in 1990, presented details, "ship biographies," of the two most important "troop ships" commandeered by the government for the task force: CANBERRA and QE2. William Flayhart [155] wrote an article on the QE2 during her time of requisition, 4 May to 11 June. Peninsular & Orient published an impressive magazine-type format, edited by John Moxworthy [369], illustrating the 94 days in which CANBERRA was utilized. Information about Canberra, her conversion, and use, can be found in Neil McCart, TWENTIETH-CENTURY PASSENGER SHIPS OF THE P & O [552].

The "advanced" base turned out to be Ascension Island, a possession of Great Britain but leased to the United States. It was 3300 miles from the Falklands/Malvinas. Duff Hart-Davis [226] recounted the history of Ascension Island, sometimes used as a cable and wireless station. Victor Flintham [156] reviewed post–World War II air operations. The United States had built a 10,000-foot runway, Wideawake Field, which was managed under contract to Pan American Airways. The British were provided maximum use. Normally 3 movements a week occurred; at the height of the campaign there were 400 per day!

Chapter 8

PUBLICATIONS AND THE MEDIA

OFFICIAL INVESTIGATIONS, REPORTS, AND STUDIES OF THE CAMPAIGN

Investigations, studies, and reports on the campaign were a common feature of both sides: the economic potential of the region, the failure of diplomacy, the failure of intelligence, military incompetence, corruption, government censorship, relations between the media and the armed forces, and sensational events such as the BELGRANO affair. Some of these investigations have been discussed elsewhere, e.g., SHACKLETON I [452] and II [453] on economic potential and another on aspects of the BELGRANO sinking.

The British investigation most remarked about and cited was the FRANKS REPORT [168] or FALKLAND ISLANDS REVIEW: REPORT OF A COMMITTEE OF PRIVY COUNSELLORS. The committee, headed by Lord Joseph Franks, concentrated its study on the period from 1965 to 2 April 1982, so no assessment of military operations was included. The various evaluations of British actions and inactions constituted an indictment, but the final conclusion was that the Thatcher government was not responsible for the Junta's decision to invade. The report cited error after error of the series of governments, of the Foreign Office, and of Parliament. The power and effectiveness of the Falklands Lobby was noted. There was no dissent from other parties.

The equivalent to the Franks study for Argentina was the RATTENBACH REPORT [422], named for General Benjamin Rattenbach and headed by Air Force Commodore Ruben O. Moro. It was an official investigation of the campaign initiated by the Argentine government. It was kept secret but certain excerpts were leaked to the press.

Latin American Newsletters published THE FALKLANDS WAR: THE OFFICIAL HISTORY, OFFICIAL COMMUNIQUES [311] CONFLICTO MALVINAS by Informe Oficial Ejercito Argentino [260] was an official report on army activities during the war. Similarly, Carlos Turolo's ASI LUCHARON [496] was a semi-official report of army actions or inactions. Admiral Jorge Fraga [167] called for the cessation of "endless rounds of negotiations" as chairman of Islas Malvinas Institute, a quasi-military agency.

Carlos Turolo also edited MALVINAS: TESTIMONIO DE SU GOBERNADOR [497], the transcript of a long interview with the military commander on the islands, General Mario B. Menendez. This apology stressed the lack of preparation and planning time—the original designated date was moved up by several months. He claimed he was uninformed about many aspects and that his recommendations were often ignored.

Rene Luria has conducted an unofficial assessment of the consequences of the conflict for Argentina in the INTERNATIONAL DEFENSE REVIEW of 1990 [322]. Military dictatorship and the Falklands/Malvinas campaign exaggerated the economic problems of inflation and debt. The defense budget was drastically cut. He then focused on the navy. The heroism of its pilots and the marines saved its honor. The remaining Super Etendards were delivered and were soon capable of carrier operations. There were ambitious plans for additional modern submarines and destroyers.

On the British side, several committees of the House of Commons undertook ongoing investigations, notably the Defence

Committee [249, 250] and the Foreign Affairs Committee [251, 252, 253]. The Foreign Affairs Committee, Session 1982–1983, investigated several matters related to the diplomacy and disposition of the Falkland Islands [253].

The matters of information, press relations, and the armed forces provoked several investigations. One of these involved relations between the media and the armed forces. The study of the Defence Committee of the House of Commons, Session 1982–1983, concluded with a two-volume report published in early December 1982, entitled "The Handling of Press and Public Information during the Falklands Conflict" [249, 250]. The media had complained of excessive censorship, "D–Notices," "off-the-record" briefings, inadequate facilities for communication, and other limitations. The Ministry of Defence was responsible for all military information matters. The Study Group on Censorship chaired by General Sir Hugh Beach was appointed well after the fact by the government to investigate such subjects in a considered, thorough manner. The 100-page report, THE BEACH REPORT [27] or THE PROTECTION OF MILITARY INFORMATION, was published in December 1983 [27, cmnd. 9112]. Innovations such as telex, satellites, alternative and more complex types of newspapers, and encryption were discussed. Specific recommendations were made concerning commentaries by retired officers and experts. The government officially responded [28, cmnd. 9499] in April 1984.

Other reports were made in several formats. John Nott, former secretary of state for defence, issued a White Paper to Parliament, an edited version of which was published in PROCEEDINGS OF THE NAVAL INSTITUTE [386]. The report was mostly a review of pertinent events and statistics. The Ministry of Defence issued individual assessments of the services, e.g., achievements of the navy [350] and operations of the army [348]. Similarly, Sir Jeremy Moore and Sir John Woodward, the campaign land and naval commanders, respectively, made presentations to RUSI, published in JRUSI [355]. They addressed issues such as Rules of Engagement, Exclusion Zones, media relations, and the BEL-GRANO sinking.

In the traditional fashion, Admiral Sir John Fieldhouse, the overall commander, published "Despatches" in supplements to

THE LONDON GAZETTE [321], e.g., 8 October and 13 December 1982. These described the operations and cited appropriate personnel for honors and awards. For example, there were 140 of these in the supplement of 8 October.

THE "RUSH-TO-PUBLICATION" PHENOMENON

Public interest in the Falklands/Malvinas conflict was extraordinarily high in Great Britain, Argentina, the United States, and elsewhere. There was, therefore, a great demand for news and information about the campaign and its operations. On the British side were serious limitations. There were few live pictures during the entire campaign. Access to communications lines was limited and there were delays in print and oral media. The Argentines were accused of overestimating British losses and exaggerating their exploits. Masses of materials were published and broadcast.

"Instant history" was a term used to describe much of the flood of publications by journalists and others in Argentina and Great Britain recounting the Falklands/Malvinas campaign. Six British reporters assigned to the task force wrote or collaborated on books. One reviewer [225, p. vi] noted, "Never in the field of human conflict has so much been written by so many so quickly."

"Victory in the Falklands" was the special picture supplement published by the PORTSMOUTH NEWS [410] in June 1982. Even before the war was over, Christopher Dobson [131] and a group of journalists brought out a book on the conflict. It was not a considered, mature effort. Leo Kanaf, LA BATALLA DE LAS MALVINAS [282], was published in August. One reviewer who was not complimentary described it as a hasty "scissor-and-paste" compilation. "Hundreds of dead" British soldiers were depicted aboard SIR GALAHAD. John Beattie [29] of the DAILY STAR circulated a "dramatic account of how a Task Force of 101 ships sailed into action 8,000 miles from home" in a magazine format at a cost of one pound. Mike Critchley edited a two-part magazine pictorial, FALKLANDS TASK FORCE PORTFOLIO [111], published immediately after the campaign. Manfred Schonfeld [450] collected a series of articles he had written for the noted Argentine newspaper LA PRENSA. These were mostly opinionated narratives with much nationalist rhetoric. Some truly outstanding colored photographs were included in the SUNDAY EXPRESS MAGAZINE Team [476] collection published in a magazine-format but with a hard cover. The publishers, Ian Allan and RUSI, jointly brought out "The Falklands Operation" [149], a photographic record and supplement to ARMED FORCES MAGAZINE. A large picture book supported by a broad—too broad and too wide-ranging—summary and review of the war was edited by Mark Dartford [120].

The prolific writer of military history, John Laffin, who has published at least 50 books, rushed to publish his interpretation, FIGHT FOR THE FALKLANDS!: WHY AND HOW BRITAIN AND ARGENTINA WENT TO WAR—FROM INVASION TO SURRENDER [306], published in September 1982. Touting "inside knowledge," the book had no table of contents, no footnotes, no bibliography, and no index. All of the signs of haste and superficiality were there.

MORE CONSIDERED, REFLECTIVE ACCOUNTS
BY JOURNALISTS

Max Hastings was the journalist-participant on the British side who became well known and highly respected during and after the campaign. He was designated "Reporter of the Year for 1982." His history, in collaboration with Simon Jenkins [229], has been much acclaimed. There was a Spanish translation [228] and at least six printings between 1983 and 1986. Hastings covered military operations and Jenkins covered domestic politics. There was an indictment of the handling of the "media war" (pp. 331–34).

Paul Eddy [137] headed the SUNDAY TIMES INSIGHT TEAM, a total of 24 writers and researchers. They produced the first complete British book-length account in September 1982, followed shortly by the Patrick Bishop–John Witherow [52] team. The Insight Team saw the war as reviving sagging British consciousness and creating the "Falklands factor" for the Conservative government. Two journalists of the task force who went ashore with the commando groups were Patrick Bishop of the OBSERVER and John Witherow of the TIMES. Their WINTER WAR [52] presented eyewitness summaries of operations, mostly ashore. Another team of collaborators was Brian Hanrahan and Robert Fox who produced "I COUNTED THEM ALL OUT AND I COUNTED THEM ALL BACK" [222]. Robert Fox of BBC Radio alone wrote EYEWITNESS FALKLANDS [166]. He won the Master of the British Empire (MBE) during the campaign for helping to negotiate the surrender at Goose Green, the only journalist to be cited. In EYEWITNESS he was successful in portraying the realities of the ground war.

Hugo Gambini [187] edited three volumes of documents having to do with the history, the war, and accounts of it, over 1100 pages with many illustrations. DON'T CRY FOR ME, SERGEANT MAJOR by Robert McGowan and Jeremy Hands [324] was part journalist impressions and part oral history. The two journalists published their notes from their observations and interviews with British forces members. Lawrence Freedman [175] described it as "a trivial pot-boiler."

A review of this type of writing was presented by Christopher Wain for THE LISTENER [513] a year after the campaign. Wain picked the Hastings-Jenkins account [229] as best and also praised the Paul Eddy, SUNDAY TIMES INSIGHT TEAM [137] effort, particularly the drawings and maps. The Bishop-Witherow WINTER WAR [52] account was written in haste.

Some have observed that there was a second surge of publications beginning in the late 1980s. Examples were G. M. Dillon [129] and Virginia Gamba-Stonehouse [183, 186].

ORAL HISTORY ACCOUNTS

Journalism was the basis for many of the early surveys of the Falklands/Malvinas campaign. The historian's method provided the model for another approach. Oral history accounts and published interviews with participants abounded from both sides.

The commendable efforts of Daniel Kon [298, 300] have been cited elsewhere (pp. 84–85). His oral history of the conscripts was among the best examples from the Argentine side. Martin Balza [17] published excerpts from about 30 interviews with Argentine soldiers at all levels.

The oral history most commented upon on the British side

was the poignant compilation of the letters of Lieutenant David Tinker, RN, A MESSAGE FROM THE FALKLANDS [488]. There was a Spanish translation [487]. Tinker was killed aboard GLA-MORGAN, hit by an EXOCET on 12 June, only two days before the end. Tinker's father published the letters of this naval veteran who had entered the service in 1975. The letters clearly demonstrated the making of an opponent of the war. Tinker often recalled historical background, e.g., Oliver Cromwell and Rupert Brooke, and increasingly during the course of the war, Tinker, and apparently his father, too, came to see the war as pointless and unjust, only perpetrated to salvage the political reputations of "the two dictators," Thatcher and Nott. He foresaw a future "fortress Falklands." The father, Hugh Tinker [489], published a commemoration on the occasion of the third anniversary, 14 June 1985, and again concluded that the war was all politics and a waste.

An important and comprehensive oral history was SPEAKING OUT: UNTOLD STORIES FROM THE FALKLANDS WAR by Michael Bilton and Peter Kosminsky [50]. They produced a TV documentary, "The Falklands War: The Untold Story," which synthesized 87 interviews of a wide variety of participants and civilians. The book included excerpts of interviews with the British ambassador to Argentina, the Argentine foreign minister, the commanding officer of BELGRANO, the military governor of the Falklands/Malvinas, and the commander of the San Carlos landing.

OUR FALKLANDS WAR by Geoffrey Underwood [499] consisted of numerous illustrations and compilations of interviews with participants, including some high-ranking British officers, in a magazine format. Underwood interviewed Commander C. Wreford-Brown, commanding officer of HMS CONQUEROR, which sank the BELGRANO. Max Arthur, ABOVE ALL, COURAGE [14], presented 30 individual accounts, 29 men and a woman, synthesized from 250 interviews. These included "Paras," marines, Welsh Guards, and Harrier and helicopter pilots.

GLOBE AND LAUREL: JOURNAL OF THE ROYAL MARINES [196], a house organ based at Southsea and printed since 1892, published a large number of articles by and about participants in the campaign.

ASSESSMENT OF MEDIA ACTIVITIES

The media aspects of this conflict were themselves a separate story, called by one "the media war." Problems between the government and the media began with the announcement of the assembling of the task force in early April. The navy was in charge at that time and their planners seemingly blundered into the issue, oblivious of potential problems. The army obviously had cultivated better relations with the media because of their previous operational experience in Northern Ireland.

How many, if any, and which journalists would accompany the task force were very early questions. The navy first said none but was forced to relent and admit a few, then more. Problems of censorship arose immediately. Dissemination of information was under the control of the Ministry of Defence. Apparently, there was "double-censorship," i.e., journalists' reports were first censored by task force censors and then again by censors at British headquarters. Highly sensitive "leaks" occurred which meant combat troops in action heard over their radios exactly where they were located and what they were to do that very day—in plenty of time so that the enemy was able to reinforce its forces. Max Hastings [229], a noted participant, dealt with these issues of the role of the media.

One general assessment was of note. Trevor Royle wrote WAR REPORT: THE WAR CORRESPONDENT'S VIEW OF BATTLE FROM THE CRIMEA TO THE FALKLANDS [439], essentially a history of modern English combat journalism. War correspondents were seen as "the newly invented curse to armies." In the case of the Falklands/Malvinas, Great Britain was unprepared for war. He reviewed the list of issues of controversy: who would go and how many, communications facilities, censorship, media defense consultants, "leaks," and the absence of live pictures. He praised Max Hastings, Brian Hanrahan, Robert Fox, and Kim Sabido.

There were some broad surveys of British media: Harry Henry, THE BUSINESS OF THE BRITISH PRESS [233]; Alan Hooper, THE MILITARY AND THE MEDIA [244], by a serving officer critical of the way the media was handled; Susan Greenberg [206] for the Campaign for Press and Broadcasting Freedom;

Derrik Mercer [338], whose lecture was published in JRUSI; and Sir David Nicholas [381], chairman of Independent TV News. Mercer accused the Ministry of Defence of being oversecretive and anti-media. He cited an instance of the Vulcan bombings of the Stanley airfield. The authorities did not want the role of the Vulcan revealed, but a bureaucrat in London leaked the information, making the ban appear to be overly restrictive. Nicholas complained that while the Ministry of Defence was restricting the British media it was supplying banned information to American papers.

It was the "yellow journalism," the sensationalized instances, which received most attention. Recall that the competition for news was fierce, especially among the London-based press, which was essentially the national press. Problems began immediately upon the announcement of the sending of the task force. Highly controversial machinations ensued. There were examples of the most sensational journalism: the notorious SUN headline, "GOT-CHA!," after BELGRANO was torpedoed, and, interestingly from the same newspaper, "Stick This Up Your Junta!"

The SUN of London was singled out as the most notable case and it has been the subject of a 1990 study, STICK IT UP YOUR PUNTER!: THE RISE AND FALL OF "THE SUN," by Peter Chippindale and Chris Horrie [93]. Among the most sensational episodes was the "GOTCHA!" headline reporting the BELGRANO sinking on 3 May—in fairness to editors of THE SUN, it should be admitted that that headline was withdrawn on subsequent editions. It was replaced with "Did 1200 Argies Drown?" And there was the made-up "INVASION" headline several days before the recapture of South Georgia, an event which presumably legitimized the false endeavor. The title headline, "Stick It Up Your Punter!," was a colloquial admonition to the Argentine leadership. A variation was "Stick This Up Your Junta!," in the SUN of 1 May 1982.

Robert Harris, GOTCHA!: THE MEDIA, THE GOVERNMENT, AND THE FALKLAND CRISIS [225], investigated the media and the war. He described it as the inside story of how Whitehall, Fleet Street, and the broadcasters went to war, not with Argentina but with each other. The BBC accused the Ministry of Defence of management and manipulation of the news. In addition to instances of the media denouncing the government and the government denouncing the media, the media denounced the media: the DAILY MIRROR said, "The SUN today is to journalism what Dr. Josef Goebbels was to truth."

Deborah Holmes [242] conducted an extensive investigation of government-media relations, especially the press, in the United States and Great Britain, including interviews with a large number of prominent figures. She concluded that the American press enjoyed greater power and prestige than the British press. She determined that there was great confusion and incompetence during the last days of March and early April as the British government prepared for the campaign. The army had learned better how to establish rapport with the press from their relations in Northern Ireland. The navy apparently knew little and originally was determined not to involve the media at all in their activities. The government intervened and intervened again until finally there was partial satisfaction all around. Thirty media representatives, none of whom were from foreign media, accompanied the task force. There were numerous instances of "leaks" back in London, the 2 PARA-Goose Green plans exposed by the BBC on 28 May being a notorious instance. Since the media was constrained from reporting British activities, some resorted to using Argentine media war reports. There were numerous complaints, including those of Thatcher and John Nott, about the "unpatriotic" coverage of the BBC.

In their desperation for news, the broadcast and print media made extensive use of retired military and naval experts called in to present their assessments. These were listed in an annex to Valerie Adams, THE MEDIA AND THE FALKLANDS CAMPAIGN [3, pp. 200–204]. Examples included Lord Carver, Lord Hill-Norton, Geoffrey Archer, Sir Michael Howard, Antony Preston, and even American admiral Elmo Zumwaldt. Such activities upset official planners and commanders who claimed these informed speculations jeopardized actual operations, e.g., one consultant explained in detail how a Mirage jet could shoot down a Harrier.

Valerie Adams [3] of the War Studies department, Kings College, London, wrote on these matters. She had previous experience in the Ministry of Defence and with committees of the

House of Commons. Edgar O'Ballance [389] studied the role of the media in Britain and Argentina. He noted problems of censorship and leaks among the British and censorship, propaganda, and misinformation on the part of the Argentines. Lawrence Freedman [170] took initiatives in academically investigating such aspects of the media.

The foreign correspondent for FINANCIAL TIMES since late 1981 remained in Argentina for over five years after the campaign. Jimmy Burns [66] made a number of observations: several secret operations were discussed, including extensive arms reinforcements (20 Boeing 707 loads) purchased from Libya, but not including what the Argentines wanted most, EXOCET missiles; British special forces activities in Chile with full Chilean cooperation; details on the disposition of the three Junta leaders (courts-martial of 1986 sentenced Anaya, Galtieri, and Dozo to 14, 12, and 8 years, respectively); punitive measures against 150 other officers, and intensification of the interservice accusations and recriminations.

SCHOLARLY AND ACADEMIC SURVEYS

The surveys mentioned most often under this category are the two by Martin Middlebrook, OPERATION CORPORATE: THE FALKLANDS WAR, 1982, alternate title, TASK FORCE [342] and THE FIGHT FOR THE MALVINAS: THE ARGENTINE FORCES IN THE FALKLANDS WAR [341]. The U.S. Naval War College used the former as a text in the wargame course on the Falklands/Malvinas campaign and it has been revised three times. Middlebrook, a prolific writer about modern historical events, concentrated on the military operations and was careful and thorough. The Argentine government at first refused to permit Middlebrook to enter the country. Later they (especially the navy) became more cooperative, according to Middlebrook. He interviewed over 60 officials including the captain and some crew members of BELGRANO and the naval pilots who sank SHEFFIELD and ARDENT. All of the Junta members were in jail by the time he began interviewing. Both books contain extensive and reliable statistics. The bibliographies are disappointing.

Lawrence Freedman of the Department of War Studies, King's College, London, published a considered, comprehensive evaluation in FOREIGN AFFAIRS, in the fall of 1982 [173], review articles [170], a more lengthy book-survey published in 1988 [171], and, with Virginia Gamba-Stonehouse, a prolific Argentine scholar, collaborated in a substantial analysis and synthesis, SIGNALS OF WAR: THE FALKLANDS CONFLICT OF 1982 [175], which came out in 1990. They touted expertise from both perspectives and summed up the past: "The inclement and inhospitable Islands themselves never became a jewel in the British imperial crown" (p. xxxii). They admitted that the Junta were conspiracy theorists but so were Governor Rex Hunt of the Falklands and Captain Nicholas Barker of ENDURANCE. They quietly concluded that the BELGRANO torpedoing had no link to the Peruvian peace plan. Admiral Anaya had previously been characterized as the most bellicose; they distributed war initiatives equally among the three members of the Junta: Galtieri, Anaya, and Lami Dozo. Virginia Gamba-Stonehouse alone published several books: MALVINAS: CONFIDENCIAL [183], LA CUESTION Y LA CRISIS [181], EL PEON DE LA REINA [184], THE FALKLANDS/MALVINAS WAR: MODEL FOR NORTH-SOUTH CRISIS PREVENTION [182] in which she called for more effective communications between the two spheres, THE SOUTH ATLANTIC CONFLICT: AN ARGENTINE VIEW [185], and STRATEGY IN THE SOUTHERN OCEANS: A SOUTH AMERICAN VIEW [186].

In his memoirs, A.J.P. Taylor [477], the well-known historian, apologized for some pieces he did for THE LISTENER. In one which he wrote at the time of the invasion, he said he condemned the Argentines with a patriotic fervor worthy of Thatcher or Michael Foot, the Labour leader. By the time of the next column he had condemned the war utterly, he said.

Over a hundred British authors and intellectuals responded to questions about the conflict in a compilation by Cecil Woolf and Jean Wilson [532].

Chapter 9

CONCLUSIONS

THE "FALKLANDS FACTOR" IN
BRITISH POLITICS

The "Falklands factor" was a matter of much political comment during the conflict and for a long time thereafter. Margaret Thatcher had emerged successfully from some obscurity during an intra-party political struggle in the Conservative party in the mid-1970s. Former prime minister Ted Heath was the loser. She was named prime minister in the election of 1979, and her reputation appeared to be sagging during the early 1980s. Fortunately for her at the time, the opposition Labourites, Social Democrats, and Liberals were hopelessly divided.

A continuing debate over the validity of the "Falklands factor" took place in the BRITISH JOURNAL OF POLITICAL SCIENCE. Harold Clarke [95] was convinced it was a major influence on the popularity of the Conservative party and insisted other variables failed to eliminate the Falklands effect. By contrast David Sanders, Hugh Ward, and David Marsh [443], in a reassessment, argued that there was little change in government popularity due to the war. The dramatic revival of its political fortunes was due to "improved macro-economic management." They presented charts and statistical tables to demonstrate that the "Falklands factor" had been "substantially overestimated" (pp. 281-82).

In July 1982 Norman Gelb [193] insisted that the "Falklands factor" had transformed British politics. Only the far Left had opposed the war. Peter Jenkins [270] questioned its validity. He contended that the government had begun regaining popularity before the spring of 1982. The "bubble" of the Social Democrat–Liberal Alliance, with a 50% support factor in December 1981, had burst by March 1982 down to 30%, and to 24% in July. The comparisons were as follows: each of the three parties had 33% in March 1982; in July, Conservative, Labour, Alliance had 46, 27, 24; in the 1983 election they had 49, 31, 16 respectively.

"FORTRESS FALKLANDS"

What now? What did the campaign accomplish? There was no armistice, no treaty, and no resolution of the problem. The sovereignty issue was as volatile and provocative as it ever had been before. After 74 days of warfare there was no answer to the Falklands/Malvinas question.

A House of Commons Defence Committee studied the future disposition and reported to the 1982–1983 session in May 1983 [248]. H.M.G. Bond [54] described activities of the weeks immediately after the resumption of British rule including details—excessive details—on repairs, deactivation of minefields, and plans for the enlarged airport. General Sir Hugh Beach, initiator of the earlier BEACH REPORT [27], wrote a dispassionate survey of BRITISH DEFENCE POLICY AND THE SOUTH ATLANTIC [26] in 1986.

THE FALKLANDS AFTERMATH: PICKING UP THE PIECES by Edward Fúrsdon [180], defence correspondent of the DAILY TELEGRAPH who only visited the Falklands/Malvinas after the war, assessed what he observed from a six-week visit. The new Mount Pleasant airfield was completed at a cost of 350 million pounds. Thatcher had visited, and the Falkland Islands Development Corporation had been launched. Similarly, Robert Fox [165], the BBC journalist-participant, returned and took a cruise on ENDURANCE in 1984. He noted the expanded military and economic build-ups and asked how it all fit into the wider context of international relations in the South Atlantic.

Peter Beck [42] described a proposed plan of settlement of the question and an update on Argentine reaction [41]. In May 1985 on the occasion of the formal opening of the new Mount Pleasant airfield, Argentina denounced the militarization of the South Atlantic, calling "Fortress Falklands" a potential NATO base. The statement concluded with the vow that Argentina would never abandon its claim. Brenda Lewis [317] noted that the Falklands had been transformed from a neglected colony into a heavily defended fortress. Still, to this day, she observed, there was no armistice or peace treaty.

LESSONS OF THE FALKLANDS/MALVINAS CAMPAIGN

A number of efforts have been focused on various "lessons" to be learned from aspects of the conflict. Official British government agencies produced assessments: the Defence Estimates for 1983 from the Ministry of Defence [351] cited "lessons" from the campaign and the Secretary of State for Defence White Paper [349] announced plans to replace lost equipment and reform policies based on the lessons learned.

Martin Edmonds [138] edited 11 essays of scholars who analyzed THE DEFENCE EQUATION: BRITISH MILITARY SYSTEMS, POLICY, PLANNING AND PERFORMANCES, including topics such as nuclear deterrence, civil-military relations, and the individual armed forces. Eric Grove [210], the independent consultant-historian, evaluated the Royal Navy in the Falklands/Malvinas campaign, the last demonstration of amphibious capabilities before they were demobilized. The conflict "worked its short-term magic" (p. 106) and the draw-down was halted. An ambitious destroyer-building program plus the Trident submarine commitment will be very costly.

In a series of other works Eric Grove has written specifically and generally about the Falklands/Malvinas campaign and its consequences [208, 209, 210]. The conflict saved the Royal Navy from the worst of the proposed draw-down of 1981. Sir John

Nott saw the navy as still appropriate for "out-of-area" contingencies. The 1985 White Paper of Michael Heseltine reduced personnel from 62,000 to 51,000. Submarines, including a new class of conventional ones, were to be added. In THE FUTURE OF SEAPOWER [209], which has been compared to works of A. T. Mahan and Sir Julian Corbett, Grove frequently referred to the lessons of the Falklands/Malvinas war. There was full coverage of Royal Navy operations in VANGUARD TO TRIDENT [210], including details on several secret operations and clarification of the BELGRANO episode. For the Royal Navy, the campaign was "the most remarkable and unexpected event of the postwar era," including the greatest losses and greatest success (p. 357).

A year after the campaign, in April 1983, in Dallas, Texas, an academically oriented conference was conducted focusing on "lessons" of the war; the proceedings were edited by James Brown [62]. From the various papers, the following conclusions were reached: the outcome was seen as a success for the volunteer-professionalized force over the conscript-inexperienced force; British forces evidenced high levels of experience and motivation; in logistical management, the Argentines built up stockpiles but failed to facilitate distribution; the British demonstrated extraordinary initiative and improvisation, drawing heavily on civilian resources; and both governments managed to maintain very high levels of public support. In September 1990, a similar conference of assessment was held at the University of Keele with many participants as presenters. The proceedings will be published in 1992, edited by Alex Danchev [544].

Norman Friedman [177] wrote on the lessons: for Argentina, the lack of interservice cooperation was fatal and the performance of army officers in failure to stay with their men was deplorable; for Great Britain, the Royal Navy was ill-suited for war in the South Atlantic and the government was plagued by problems of secrecy. Anthony Cordesman penned two accounts [106, 107] reviewing the lessons from Argentine and British perspectives, diplomatic and operational. Lawrence Freedman [172] wrote on future British defence policy. Other analysts included John Moore for JANE'S NAVAL REVIEW [356] and the International Institute for Strategic Studies [263]. For example, Moore noted that quick-firing guns were being added to Type 22 frigates, previously

configured only with missiles. In a 1989 article John Jordan
[278] was disappointed that the promised additional destroyers,
aircraft carriers, and amphibious ships were not being ordered.
In SOMEONE HAD BLUNDERED: A HISTORICAL SURVEY OF
MILITARY INCOMPETENCE, Geoffrey Regan [426] mentioned
Goose Green.
John Baylis [24] edited a series of nine essays written after
the war and assessed its consequences. It was "a close run
thing" (p. 23), concluded Baylis. Six British ships were sunk
but 10 more were hit by bombs that did not explode; 16 of
23 major warships could have been lost. There were essays by
Lawrence Freedman (pp. 62–75), Lord Carver (pp. 76–91), and
Lord Hill-Norton (pp. 117–37).
Still others were Americans pointing to the lessons to be
learned for the United States: Admiral Thomas Moorer and
Alvin Cottrell [360], Admiral Stansfield Turner [495], Commander
Bruce Watson and Colonel Peter Dunn [517], and Gabriel Marcella
[328]. The lessons included such observations as that the foot
soldier was still the final decisive contributor to victory and that
attack aircraft carriers were needed to fill essential gaps. The
U.S. Navy appointed a study group to assess lessons. Roland
Brandquist and Michael Sidrow [58] reported in an article in PRO-
CEEDINGS. "Strengthen the Surface Navy!" was their message.
Such ships remained essential.
ANOTHER STORY: WOMEN AND THE FALKLANDS WAR
by Jean Carr [84] presented "the reverse side of the Falklands
coin," focusing on a neglected aspect of the war, the families
of the British armed forces, what Carr termed "the tragic human aftermath" (p. vii). Carr, a journalist for the SUNDAY MIR-
ROR who obviously was sympathetic and who interviewed many
members of military families in Great Britain, wrote a series of
exposes about inadequate and mismanaged provisions for the
families and the military personnel themselves during and after
the campaign. A South Atlantic Fund was created, reaching 16
million pounds, which, Carr contended, was poorly executed and
scandalously handled. Unfortunately her effort was overly shrill,
undocumented, and without scholarly apparatus.
Two Argentine socialists, Alejandro Dabat and Luis Lorenzano
[113, 114], surveyed the aftermath of the campaign and the

national crisis it precipitated. The invasion caused a split in the Left in Argentina, some seeing it as a neo-colonial country waging a just war of national liberation against imperialism and others seeing it as machinations of a bloodthirsty and reactionary dictatorship.

PROCEEDINGS OF THE NAVAL INSTITUTE [417] published "Falklands Postscripts" [150] a year after the campaign ended. An impressive group of commentators made observations, including the young Australian naval officer–scholar James Goldrick, the expert on Latin American navies Dr. Robert Scheina, and the naval annual editor A. D. Baker. Goldrick assessed British strategic doctrine over the last years as "gravely flawed," but he praised the timely initiatives of the forces and the decisiveness and persistence of the prime minister.

Several events are planned in anticipation of the tenth anniversary of the campaign. THE ROAD TO WAR, a British Broadcasting Corporation television documentary series [553], is preparing a four-part piece, "The Falklands Conflict." Ann Hills [549] recounted some upcoming occasions to be celebrated at Port Stanley: the opening of a new museum, the tenth anniversary of the campaign, and the quatracentennial of the discovery of the Falklands by John Davis in 1592.

Chapter 10

CULTURE

FICTION, VIDEOS, MOVIES, DRAMA, ART, AND EXHIBITIONS

The Falkland/Malvinas Islands and the campaign were the topics of some "culture," i.e., creative efforts of various genres and modes of the fine arts. There were a number of examples.

Well-known pieces of classical fictional literature have been identified with the region of the South Atlantic and the islands: Samuel Taylor Coleridge's THE RIME OF THE ANCIENT MARINER [96], a lyrical ballad published in 1798, was set in the region, and Daniel Defoe's ROBINSON CRUSOE [126], the story of 1719 inspired by the adventures of Alexander Selkirk, a Scottish sailor marooned on a remote island, might have taken place on the Falklands/Malvinas.

In the literary genre of "spy adventures," James Bond, the fictional British agent "007" created by Ian Fleming and continued by John Gardner [189] after the death of Fleming, participated in unspecified secret operations during the Falklands campaign.

Recall that there were very few live pictures of events available to the British public at all during the course of the campaign. The

British public and others demanded and received video coverage afterward. Under the category of "video," compiled color films of aspects of the campaign, several have been produced and are available for sale to the general public, e.g., from Fusion Video, Tinley Park, Illinois. "Battle for the Falklands" [23] was a video of 110 minutes, an edited collection of the best film news coverage. Footage from the British flagship, HERMES, was produced as "Falklands: Task Force South" [151], a video of 120 minutes. Antony Preston, a noted expert commentator on military affairs, wrote and produced "The West's Fighting Ships" [414], a 60–minute video demonstrating graphically the capabilities of navies of the West.

A quasi-official documentary by Ian Curteis, THE FALKLANDS PLAY: A TELEVISION PLAY [112], was produced and published in 1987. After much haggling with the government, a three-hour performance was planned for BBC-1 for 2 April 1987, but it was never shown. Some sensational features, ascertainable in the published narrative, were "Haigspeak," the convoluted language used by the American secretary of state, and Galtieri's drunkenness. Another BBC-TV play was "When the Fighting Is Over: A Personal Story of the Battle of Tumbledown Mountain and Its Aftermath" by John and Robert Lawrence [313], a fictionalized version. There was little critical praise for it. Plans for a tenth anniversary television documentary, "The Falklands Conflict," a four-part contribution in THE ROAD TO WAR series [553], have been described elsewhere.

Efforts under the category of drama included the following. "Falkland Sound/Voces de Malvinas" [148] was a play performed at the Royal Theatre during the summer of 1983. Steven Berkoff wrote "Sink the BELGRANO!, with Massage" [49], which was, in fact, two plays, the former being pertinent. It was performed at two theaters in the fall of 1986. A play depicting a consequence of the Ponting Affair, "Who Killed Hilda Murrell?" [524], was produced at the Tricycle Theatre, London, in May 1986.

Related endeavors were produced in Argentina. Rodolfo Fogwill, LOS PICHY-CYEGOS: VISIONES DE UNA BATALLA SUBTERRANEA [157], was an original satire on the war based on conversations with families. Daniel Kon and Bebe Kamin [299] made a film from Kon's best-selling LOS CHICOS DE

LA GUERRA [298] about the deplorable state of the Argentine conscripts. It was shown at the London Film Festival of 1984. NO HABRA MAS PENAS NI OLVIDO (translation, A FUNNY DIRTY LITTLE WAR) by Osvaldo Soriano [464, 465] was a published play which viciously attacked the Argentine military and especially the Peronists. Neither was at all amused at being depicted as villains in a sleepy little town reeking with political corruption. This first came out in Spain in 1980, and more appropriately, after 1982 in Argentina. An English version [464] was published in 1986. LAS MALVINAS: TRAGICOMEDIA EN TRES ACTOS by Gralalberto Muller Rojas [434] was a published play of 1983. Juan Jose Jusid made two movies [280, 281], allegories of past events to raise the political consciousness of contemporary Argentines.

Painted art works were also included. Linda Kitson was the official artist for the campaign. She has written a "visual diary" [296], and there has been an exhibition [295] of 94 of her drawings at the Imperial War Museum, November 1982. It then went on tour. John Hamilton [221] told the story of helicopters in the Falklands/Malvinas campaign in paintings, spending four years there researching and identifying sites. The artist R. G. Smith [460] produced a colorful and realistic depiction of "Bomb Alley" on 21 May when Argentine A-4s bombed two Type 21 frigates, sinking HMS ARDENT, while the Argentines lost two A-4s. A print can be obtained from N. B. Fine Arts of Torrance, California for $45.00. This picture was used for the double-page folding cover of PROCEEDINGS [417] for May 1983.

THE "PHILATELIC" FACTOR

Postage stamps, an aspect of "culture," have had their uses in the unfolding of the issues and conflicts described in this book. In addition, through uses of manipulation of visas and passports, of cartography, and of postage stamps, countries involved can convey political messages and policy statements.

Robert Burns [19, 540], James Andrews [538], and Bernard Grant [205] were among the authors writing about the unique postal services of the Falklands/Malvinas. J.N.T. Howat [254] wrote of FALKLAND ISLANDS MAILS and a Hamburg enterprise. Andrew Norris and David Beech [384], stamp auctioneers, described "Travis" franks and covers associated with the Falklands/Malvinas.

The Kelpers were not alone in manipulating postage stamp propaganda. As Peter Beck [37] noted, in 1936 Argentina issued a one-peso stamp illustrating southern South America. Interestingly the Falkland/Malvinas Islands and large sections of the southwest appear in the same color as that of Argentina. Chile complained and the stamp was reissued "correcting" the southwestern boundaries. In 1964 and in 1976 stamps were issued depicting the Falklands/Malvinas, South Georgia, and South Sandwich islands, none of which, of course, were Argentine territory.

Chapter 11

RESEARCH

ARCHIVES, RECORD OFFICES, LIBRARIES, AND READING ROOMS

Most of the events recounted in this narrative have occurred so recently that there has been insufficient time for many of the traditional primary sources to accumulate: government documents, official records, memoirs, diaries, letters, personal papers, and even biographies, though there have been a few of those, e.g., Carrington [86], Haig [218], Weinberger [521], and many of the journalists.

In Great Britain the "Thirty-Year Rule" applies. That means that under the regulations of official secrets and other guidelines, official and especially classified information will not be available to researchers and the public until after 2012.

Nevertheless, there are several research sites in Great Britain and in Argentina where official documents and published government papers and many other pertinent official and primary sources can be accessed. The diplomatic story, for example, can be researched in these centers. Such places in Great Britain included the Public Record Office, the largest official repository of all government records in Great Britain. Records such as those of the Foreign Office and Ministry of Defence would be found at Kew, on the Thames River. There is a Ministry of Defence Library and Reading Rooms at the National Maritime and Imperial War Museums. The most extensive library in Great Britain is the British Library, formerly the British Museum Library, in London. In the United States, the equivalents would be the National Archives and the Library of Congress, both in Washington, D.C. The equivalent national archival centers are available in Argentina.

JOURNALS, PERIODICALS, MAGAZINES, AND NEWSPAPERS

The Falklands/Malvinas campaign was extraordinarily popular both in the countries involved and in most of the world, e.g., in the rest of Latin America, in Europe, in the Commonwealth and Dominion states, and in the Third World generally. Thus, the immediate, daily, and weekly media were anxious to provide extensive and up-to-date coverage of all important events associated with the campaign, and they did so. In a historiographical and bibliographical survey of mostly secondary publications such as this, it would be impossible to include all pertinent items in newspapers, popular magazines, and service journals.

However, articles of a more reflective nature in professional journals and periodicals, weekly, monthly, and quarterly intellectual and academic journals, and professional military, naval, and air journals would be germane and, in fact, have been incorporated in the bibliography. An inordinate number of high-quality journals and periodicals published running commentaries on the activities of the campaign. A survey and summary of some of these types of publications follows.

> AEREOSPACIO/AEROSPACE: REVISTA NACIONALAE-RONAUTICA Y ESPACIAL [4]. A bi-monthly professional journal since 1931. Buenos Aires. Text in Spanish and English.
> AVIATION WEEK AND SPACE TECHNOLOGY [16]. A weekly professional magazine since 1916. New York.

DEFENCE [125]. A monthly journal since 1970. Redhill, Surrey. It devoted a special issue, November 1982, to the campaign.

THE ECONOMIST [136]. A weekly professional newspaper since 1843. London.

HARPER'S MAGAZINE [224]. A monthly magazine since 1850.

INTELLIGENCE AND NATIONAL SECURITY [261]. A quarterly periodical since 1986. London.

INTERNATIONAL AFFAIRS [262]. A quarterly review for the Royal Institute of International Affairs since 1922. Guilford, England.

LA PRENSA [309]. Daily newspaper of Buenos Aires.

MILLENNIUM: JOURNAL OF INTERNATIONAL STUDIES [345]. A quarterly journal since 1971, London: London School of Economics. It devoted an entire issue (Spring 1983) to the question, three of the seven articles being on the sovereignty issue.

NAVAL HISTORY [375]. A quarterly popular history journal since 1987. Annapolis, MD.

NAVAL WAR COLLEGE REVIEW [377]. A quarterly journal since 1948. Newport, RI.

NEWSWEEK [379]. A weekly newsmagazine since 1933. New York.

NEW YORK REVIEW OF BOOKS [380]. A literary review, 22 times a year. New York.

PROCEEDINGS OF THE NAVAL INSTITUTE [417]. A monthly periodical since 1874. Annapolis, MD.

RUSI AND BRASSEY'S DEFENCE YEARBOOK [440]. An annual journal since 1890. London.

SIETE DIAS ILUSTRADOS [455]. A weekly review. Buenos Aires.

TIME [486]. A weekly newsmagazine since 1923. New York.

TLS: TIMES LITERARY SUPPLEMENT [490]. A weekly review of literature. London.

Appendix I

CHRONOLOGY OF EVENTS ASSOCIATED WITH THE FALKLANDS/MALVINAS CAMPAIGN

Salient dates of incidents related to the Falklands/Malvinas international dispute and the campaign were as follows:

1494 — Papal Treaty of Tordesillas, allocating these territories to be the Falkland/Malvinas Islands and all others (then unknown) west of a certain line to Spain, east of the line to Portugal.

1501–1502 — a Portuguese voyage to the South Atlantic by an unknown vessel but the pilot was Amerigo Vespucci, and it may have called at South Georgia or the Falklands/Malvinas.

1540 — ?? alleged occupation by the French; Magellan may have sighted the islands.

1592 — John Davis of HMS DESIRE discovered the islands for the English.

1594 — Richard Hawkins rediscovered the islands for the English.

1698 — the first recorded landing, by privateer John Strong in an English ship, WELFARE; the name was from the Treasurer of the Royal Navy, Viscount Falkland.

1764 — Louis de Bougainville and French colonists from St. Malo landed; about 80 persons settled.

1766 — Spain purchased the colony from France for 25,000 pounds; about the same time, Captain John Byron claimed the islands for the English.

1770 — Spanish-British in armed conflict; threat of war.

1771 — London Declaration, confirmation of the British claim.

1774 — the British departed but maintained their claim.

1800–1830s — Latin American rebellions against Spain.

1816 — Argentina claimed to have inherited Spanish possessions.

1833 — Captain Onslow of HMS CLIO arrived at the Falklands/Malvinas, expelled the Argentines occupying at that time, and claimed or reclaimed the islands for the British.

The French settlers had brought cattle and some Scots brought sheep. The cattle were all killed off; the sheep proliferated and wool became the primary commodity of the islands. In 1973 there were 630,000 sheep.

1950 — The Argentine legislature declared the Falklands/Malvinas as Argentine territory.

1959 — Antarctic Treaty.

1960 — 14 December, U.N. Resolution 1514, calling for an end of colonization.

1965 — 15 December, U.N. Resolution 2065, calling on Argentina and Great Britain to negotiate over claims to the Falkland/Malvinas Islands.

1966 — several aggressive incidents associated with the

problem, e.g., 20 young Argentines representing "Movimiento Nuena Argentina" staged "Operacion Condor" on 28 September 1966, a symbolic seizure of territory. This set back negotiations.

1971 — Anglo-Argentine Communications Agreement.

1974 — another U.N. resolution urging solution. Defence Review called for withdrawal of HMS ENDURANCE from South Atlantic.

1976 — Argentines occupy South Thule; 4 February, the "SHACKLETON" affair: the unarmed British research ship en route to the Falklands/Malvinas, when about 80 miles away, was fired upon several times by an Argentine destroyer. The British issued strenuous objections.

— Decision on ENDURANCE reversed.

— Shackleton Survey, a socio-economic study to determine future potential of the Falkland Islands and the region around it, including oil, fishing, joint endeavors with Argentina, etc.

1978 — Constantino Davidoff contracted to remove four abandoned whaling stations from South Georgia.

1980 — Nicholas Ridley made an investigative visit to the Falklands; when he returned and reported to the House of Commons, his suggestions, e.g., for a lease-back arrangement with Argentina, were shouted down, allegedly at the behest of the "Falklands Lobby."

1981 — Defence Review called for withdrawal of ENDURANCE.

1982 — the Falklands population was 1813, with 1000 of them living in Port Stanley.

3 February — British formally protested Davidoff's actions associated with South Georgia.

19 March — Davidoff's workers and a contingent of Argentine marines to South Georgia.

26 March — Argentine Junta made the decision to invade.

1 April — at 2100 hours, 80 Argentine commandos from a destroyer (a Type 42 Class, British built) landed around Port Stanley.

2 April — Argentine forces invade the Falklands; British garrison of 68 Royal Marines and Governor Rex Hunt surrender.

3 April — Argentines land at Grytviken, South Georgia, and take 86 Royal Marines and British civilians prisoner.

Resolution 502, U.N. Security Council, demanded Argentine withdrawal and a resolution of the dispute. The British diplomatic establishment exerted maximum efforts on this one: it required a two-thirds majority, and, of course, no big power vetoes. The vote was 10 for (Thatcher personally called King Hussein to persuade on the Jordan vote), 4 against (Spain, Panama, China, and Poland), with Russia abstaining.

7 April — British declared 200–mile Exclusion Zone around the Falklands.

8 April — Haig shuttle diplomacy began.

24 April — British Sea King helicopter landed in Chile.

26 April — South Georgia recovered by British forces; 180 POWs taken.

30 April — 12 British warships entered Exclusion Zone; British declared Total Exclusion Zone.

1 May — Argentine task force, including aircraft carrier operating west of British task force, prepared to launch an air attack, but the wind was insufficient and the attack was cancelled; Vulcan bomber bombed Stanley airfield.

2 May — President Belaunde Terry of Peru made a proposal for peace; BELGRANO sunk by CONQUEROR; Argentine navy withdrew to bases.

4 May — Super Etendards with EXOCET missiles attacked task force, and sank SHEFFIELD.

4 May–21 May — Argentine air attacks continued, sinking and damaging British warships. Meanwhile the task force prepared for a major amphibious landing.

21 May — British amphibious landing, Port San Carlos, East Falkland island.

27–29 May — battle of Goose Green, in which 1500 Argentines surrendered to 500 British Commandos.

30 May — alleged successful attack on INVINCIBLE.

11 June — sustained attack on Stanley began.

14 June — last Argentine forces surrender at Port Stanley.

Samuel Morison published detailed chronologies of the campaign in NIProc [364] and WARSHIP INTERNATIONAL [365].

Appendix II

GLOSSARY OF IMPORTANT PERSONS

Anaya, Admiral Jorge Isaac, Argentine navy commandant and Junta member.

Carrington, Lord Peter, foreign minister of Great Britain.

Costa Mendez, Dr. Nicanor, foreign minister of Argentina.

Davidoff, Constantino, scrap metal dealer from Buenos Aires.

Fieldhouse, Admiral Sir John, commander-in-chief, fleet and commander of Operation Corporate.

Galtieri, General, later President, Leopoldo Fortunato, army commandant and president of Argentina after December 1981.

Haig, General Alexander, secretary of state of the United States.

Kirkpatrick, Jeane J., U.S. ambassador to the United Nations.

Lami Dozo, General Arturo Bisilio, air force commandant and Junta member.

Lewin, Admiral of the Fleet Sir Terence, chief of the defence staff.

Menendez, General Mario Benjamin, military governor of the Malvinas.

Perez de Cuellar, Javier, secretary-general of the United Nations.

Thatcher, Margaret, prime minister of Great Britain.

Thompson, General Julian, commander 3 Commando.

Weinberger, Caspar, secretary of defense of the United States.

Williams, Sir Anthony, British ambassador to Argentina.

PART II

ANNOTATED BIBLIOGRAPHY

1 Adams, Valerie. THE FALKLANDS CONFLICT. FLASH POINTS series. East Sussex: Wayland, 1988, 78 pp.
Large picture book; oriented toward juveniles; chapter on the media war, pp. 63–67.

2 Adams, Valerie. "Logistic Support for the Falklands Campaign." JRUSI, 129 (September 1984): 43–49.
Primary responsibility by the RN; details on planning, preparation, loading, restowing on Ascension Island base.

3 Adams, Valerie. THE MEDIA AND THE FALKLANDS CAMPAIGN. New York: St. Martins; London: Macmillan, 1986, 234 pp.
Foreword by Lawrence Freedman; extensive review of issues associated with media coverage; by experienced, veteran civil servant; appendix list of military commentators.

4 AEREOESPACIO/AEROSPACE: REVISTA NACIONAL AEROMAUTICA Y ESPACIAL. Bi-monthly periodical. Buenos Aires.
Series of articles throughout 1982, 1983, and 1984 on aspects of the campaign, e.g., Argentine air attacks on INVINCIBLE and rescue of downed British pilot.

5   Alemann, Roberto T. LA POLITICA ECONOMICA DURANTE EL CONFLICTO AUSTRAL. Buenos Aires: Academie Nacional de Ciencias Economicas, 1983.
Detailed account of economic policy before and during campaign.

6   Allardyce, Sir William Lamond. THE STORY OF THE FALKLAND ISLANDS: BEING AN ACCOUNT OF THEIR DISCOVERY AND EARLY HISTORY, 1500–1842. Stanley: Government Printing, 1909, 31 pp.
An old local history locally printed.

7   Andrada, Benigno Hector. GUERRA AEREA EN LAS MALVINAS. Buenos Aires: Emece Editores, 1983, 239 pp.
Argentine account of the campaign.

8   Annan, Noel. "Mrs. Thatcher's Case." NEW YORK REVIEW OF BOOKS, 29 (15 July 1982): 20–22.
Review of the background leading to the crisis; details on Ridley's "lease-back" proposal quashed by the Falklands Lobby and on some "signals."

9   Arblaster, Anthony. THE FALKLANDS: THATCHER'S WAR; LABOUR'S GUILT. London: Socialist Society, 1982.
By articulate opponent of the campaign; published while the campaign was in progress.

10   Arce, Jose. LAS MALVINAS: LAS PEQUENAS ISLAS QUE-NOS FUERON ARREBATADAS. Madrid: Instituto de Cultura Hispanica, 1950, 196 pp.
Historic background from the Argentine perspective; claimed the islands as Argentine territory since 1810; British seizure was illegal in 1833.

11   Arce, Jose. THE MALVINAS: OUR SNATCHED LITTLE ISLES. Madrid: Blass, 1951, 177 pp.
The basis of Argentine claims was "jus gentium."

12   Armitage, M. J. and Mason, R. A., eds. AIR POWER IN THE NUCLEAR AGE: THEORY AND PRACTICE. Urbana: U Illinois P; London: Macmillan, 1983, 311 pp.

Chapter by Armitage on the campaign, pp. 202–22; details on airfields—there were 31 scattered over the islands; Argentines initially enjoyed air superiority but the British slowly took over.

13 Arnstein, Walter. BRITAIN YESTERDAY AND TODAY: 1830 TO THE PRESENT. Lexington, MA: Heath, 1966, 1971, 1976, 1983, 1988, 486 pp.

A standard textbook history of modern Great Britain by a noted authority; kept up to date with new editions; campaign, pp. 422–24.

14 Arthur, Max. ABOVE ALL, COURAGE: FIRST-HAND ACCOUNTS FROM THE FALKLANDS FRONT LINE. London: Sidwick & Jackson; Sphere, 1985, 1986, 479 pp.

250 interviews of "front-line" veterans: "Paras," Welsh Guards, Royal Marines, Harrier and helicopter pilots, women; focused on 29 men and a woman.

15 Ascherson, Neal. "By San Carlos Water." LONDON REVIEW OF BOOKS, 4 (18 November 1982): 3–6.

Review article of eight publications on the campaign, e.g., P. Bishop [52], D. Kon [298], and H. Tinker [489].

16 AVIATION WEEK AND SPACE TECHNOLOGY. Weekly. New York.

Authoritative weekly professional magazine; maintained coverage on technological advances and weapons used during the campaign.

17 Balza, Martin Antonio. MALVINAS: RELATOS DE SOLDADOS. Buenos Aires: Cerculo Militar, 1985, 160 pp.

Oral history; individual accounts from 30 interviews/stories; included captain, sergeants, and soldiers.

18 Barcia Trelles, Camilo. EL PROBLEMA DE LAS ISLAS MALVINAS. Madrid: Editora Nacional, 1943, 1968, 114 pp.

An older review of the background from the Argentine perspective.

19 Barnes, Robert. THE POSTAL SERVICE OF THE FALKLAND ISLANDS: INCLUDING SOUTH SHETLANDS, 1906–

1931, AND SOUTH GEORGIA. London: Lowe, 1972, 103 pp.

An aspect of a unique feature of the Falklands/Malvinas, a source of international interest in the decades before the campaign.

20 Barnett, Anthony. "Iron Britannia." NEW LEFT REVIEW, 134 (July-August 1982): 5–96.

From a special issue on the Falklands/Malvinas question; by a noted critic of the campaign; sections on "crackpot" Parliament, Churchillism, and Thatcherism; "Falklands factor" gave "a virulent new lease on life to Margaret Thatcher's authoritarian populism."

21 Barnett, Anthony. IRON BRITANNIA. London: Allison & Busby, 1982, 160 pp.

By an outspoken opponent, written during the campaign; much concern about the lack of opposition to the campaign; chapter on the nature of public and media support; Lawrence Freedman noted that this was better organized than the critique of Tam Dalyell [115].

22 Barnett, Correlli. BRITAIN AND HER ARMY, 1509–1970: A MILITARY, POLITICAL, AND SOCIAL SURVEY. New York and London: Morrow, 1970, 549 pp.

A standard but revisionist history of the British army; excellent on background.

23 "Battle for the Falklands." Video. Tinley Park, IL: Fusion, n.d., 110 min.

A compilation of the best of the video news coverage; recall that little or no filmed action was available to the British public during the campaign.

24 Baylis, John B., ed. ALTERNATIVE APPROACHES TO BRITISH DEFENCE POLICY. London: Macmillan, 1983, 258 pp.

Nine essays; Lawrence Freedman on "After the Falklands," pp. 62–75; noted the campaign was "a close-run thing," that 16 of 23 British warships could have been sunk; Freedman [171] concluded that the surface ships were extremely vulnerable even to obsolescent weapons.

25 BBC PANORAMA programme. "Interview with Margaret Thatcher." 26 April 1982.
When the campaign was less than one month along; focus of the interview was Thatcher's insistence on the right of self-determination for the Kelpers.

26 Beach, Sir Hugh. BRITISH DEFENCE POLICY AND THE SOUTH ATLANTIC. London: South Atlantic Council Occasional Paper # 2, May 1986.
A dispassionate survey of the campaign and after by a noted expert, author of the BEACH REPORT [27].

27 Beach, Sir Hugh. BEACH REPORT. THE PROTECTION OF MILITARY INFORMATION. REPORT OF THE STUDY GROUP ON CENSORSHIP. Cmnd 9112. London: HMSO, December 1983.
Famous high-level Study Group investigation of government-media relations and censorship; report submitted to Michael Heseltine, defence minister.

28 Beach, Sir Hugh. BEACH REPORT—RESPONSE. THE PROTECTION OF MILITARY INFORMATION. Government Responseto the Report of the Study Group on Censorship. Cmnd 9499. London: HMSO, April 1984.
Response to [27].

29 Beattie, John. THE FALKLANDS STORY. London: Express Newspapers, 1982, 66 pp.
Very early survey on sale for one pound; magazine format.

30 Beaver, Paul. ATTACK HELICOPTERS. London: Arms & Armour, 1987, 144 pp.
History of this innovative aircraft which had become so essential to modern warfare; first used in Korean War, early 1950s; estimated almost 7000 in use in military forces by 1987.

31 Beaver, Paul. THE BRITISH AIRCRAFT CARRIER. Cambridge: Stevens; N.Y.: Sterling, 1982, 1984, 1987, 256 pp.
Great Britain had 52 attack carriers with 18 building in 1945; reviewed the series of major innovations originated by the British;

of course no attack carriers were available during the campaign; reviewed developments since the campaign.

32 Beaver, Paul. ENCYCLOPEDIA OF THE MODERN ROYAL NAVY: INCLUDING THE FLEET AIR ARM AND ROYAL MARINES. Cambridge: Stevens, 1982, 329 pp.
Included the campaign; much praise for the highest level of professionalism demonstrated by the RN.

33 Beaver, Paul. INVINCIBLE CLASS. MODERN COMBAT SHIPS series, # 2. London: Ian Allan, 1984, 96 pp.
Controversial class, originally to be command cruisers; three of these light carriers built: INVINCIBLE, ILLUSTRIOUS (in commission immediately after the campaign), and ARK ROYAL.

34 Beaver, Paul. THE ROYAL NAVY IN THE 1980s. New York: Sterling; London: Arms & Armour, 1985, 72 pp.
Many illustrations; a timely and comprehensive review by a noted expert.

35 Beaver, Paul. TODAY'S ROYAL MARINES. London: Stephens, 1988, 160 pp.
Especially good on post-1945 period.

36 Beck, Peter J. "The Anglo-Argentine Dispute over Title to the Falkland Islands: Changing British Perceptions on Sovereignty since 1910." MILLENNIUM, 12 (Spring 1983): 6–24.
By an international history academic; on the early history of the dispute; key doubts on the precise legal status as of January 1833; praise for the Goebel account [199].

37 Beck, Peter J. "Argentina's 'Philatelic Annexation' of the Falkland Islands in the 1930s." HISTORY TODAY, 33 (February 1983): 39–44.
The Kelpers exploited the unique "philatelic" interest, but so did the Argentines by releasing stamps illustrating the Falkland/Malvinas Islands, and even South Georgia and South Sandwich, as Argentine territory, e.g., in 1964 and 1976.

38 Beck, Peter J. "Britain's Antarctic Dimension." INTERNATIONAL AFFAIRS, 59 (Summer 1983): 429–44.

Another "signal" about the changing British interests in the South Atlantic; a tendency to lose interest in the British Antarctic Survey in 1982, but this was reversed after the campaign.

39 Beck, Peter J. "Cooperative Confrontation in the Falkland Islands Dispute: The Anglo-Argentina Search for a Way Forward, 1968–1981." JOURNAL OF INTER-AMERICAN STUDIES, 24 (February 1982): 37–56.

Written before the campaign; noted Falklands/Malvinas problem followed the pattern of Latin American disputes: inability to compromise causing deterioration of relationships, difficult to resolve, and complexities over the issue of sovereignty.

40 Beck, Peter J. THE FALKLAND ISLANDS AS AN INTERNATIONAL PROBLEM. New York and London: Routledge, 1988, 1989, 223 pp.

A recent and timely synthesis of the issues; noted some past incidents, e.g., Shackleton affair of 1976 as the most serious one prior to 1982.

41 Beck, Peter J. "Falklands or Malvinas?: The View from Buenos Aires." CONTEMPORARY REVIEW, 247 (September 1985): 136–42.

On the occasion of the opening of the new Mount Pleasant airfield, prompted renewed interest and denunciation from Argentine officials, accusing the British of provocation: "Fortress Falklands" as a potential NATO base!; Argentines again vowed never to abandon claim.

42 Beck, Peter J. "The Future of the Falkland Islands: A Solution Made in Hong Kong." INTERNATIONAL AFFAIRS, 6 (Autumn 1985): 643–60.

Reference to one of several proposed resolutions.

43 Beck, Peter J. THE INTERNATIONAL POLITICS OF ANTARCTICA. London: Croom Helm, 1986, 332 pp.

On the role of Antarctica in international politics; a series of conferences and seminars, accelerated the processes after 1982.

44 Becu, Ricardo Zorraquin. INGLATERRA PROMETIO ABANDONAR LAS MALVINAS. Buenos Aires: Platero, 1975.

Pre-campaign review of Argentine claims.

45 Belgrano Action Group. THE UNNECESSARY WAR: PRO-
CEEDINGS OF THE BELGRANO ENQUIRY, NOVEMBER 7–8,
1986. Nottingham: Spokesman, 1988, 184 pp.
Recounted "war-crimes-trial" proceedings in 1986, Hamstead
Town Hall, when prominent persons such as Tam Dalyell denounced the government for cover-up and a conscious effort to
quash certain peace proposals.

46 Benn, Tony. TONY BENN ON THE FALKLANDS WAR.
SPOKESMAN PAMPHLET # 79. Nottingham: Bertrand Russell
Place, 1982, 15 pp.
By a vocal critic of the government and the campaign; included
his speech in the debate of 6 April, but Benn failed to persuade
Labour to oppose the campaign.

47 Bennett, Geoffrey Martin. CORONEL AND THE FALK-
LANDS. BRITISH BATTLES series. London: Batsford; New York:
Macmillan, 1962, 192 pp.
A standard account with new information; claims to be the
first comprehensive account since the official history 40 years
previously.

48 Berger, Martin. EL RESCATE DE LAS MALVINAS. Lanus
Oeste: Bruguera, 1982, 210 pp.
Included historical background of Argentine invasion opera-
tions.

49 Berkoff, Steven. "Sink the BELGRANO!, with Massage." A
Play. London: Faber, 1987, 63 pp.
A dramatic portrayal critical of the campaign; Tam Dalyell
[116] opened as "the still small voice of truth"; Berkoff noted
the influence of the Gavshon-Rice work [92]; cast included "Maggot Scratcher," "Pimp," and "Nit"; "Massage" was a second
unrelated play.

50 Bilton, Michael and Kosminsky, Peter. SPEAKING OUT:
UNTOLD STORIES FROM THE FALKLANDS WAR. London:
Deutsch, 1989, 311 pp.

Oral history; 87 TV interviews of participants, e.g., General Julian Thompson, Rick Jolly, foreign minister Nicanor Costa Mendez, commanding officer of the BELGRANO, British ambassador Williams, and military governor Menendez.

51 Bingham, E. Barry S. FALKLANDS, JUTLAND AND THE BIGHT. London: Murray, 1919, 155 pp.

By commander, RN, a participant in all three battles; introduction by Admiral Sir David Beatty; reviewed three important naval battles of World War I.

52 Bishop, Patrick Joseph and Witherow, John. THE WINTER WAR: THE FALKLANDS. New York and London: Quartet, 1982, 152 pp.

By journalists-veterans of the campaign, Bishop of the OBSERVER and Witherow of the TIMES; recounted personal observations of operations; no analysis or mature reflections.

53 Bologna, Alfred Bruno. "Argentinian Claims to the Malvinas under International Law." MILLENNIUM, 12 (Spring 1983): 39–48.

A detailed diplomatic review stressing Argentine positions.

54 Bond, H.M.G. "The Historian and the Falklands Aftermath." ARMY QUARTERLY AND DEFENCE JOURNAL, 119 (April 1989): 151–52.

Review of Fursdon book [180].

55 Bougainville, Louis-Antoine de. VOYAGE AUTOUR DE MONDE PAR LA FREGATE DU ROI, 1766–1769. 2 vols. Paris: Saillard & Nyon, 1771, 1772.

Lengthy memoirs of famous French explorer during voyage around the world, including a call at the Falklands/Malvinas Islands.

56 Bougainville, Louis-Antoine de. A VOYAGE ROUND THE WORLD. London: J. Nourse, 1772.

Translated by J. R. Forster; English version of [55].

57 Boyson, V. F. THE FALKLAND ISLANDS: WITH NOTES ON THE NATURAL HISTORY BY RUPERT VALLENTIN. Oxford: Clarendon, 1924, 426 pp.

Early history, from about 1600 to 1850s; on the natural life and
geophysical conditions.

58 Brandquist, Roland and Sidrow, Michael R. "Falkland Fall-
out: Strengthen the Surface Navy!" NIProc, 110 (July 1984):
132–37.
By members of the Falkland Islands Study Group of the U.S.
Navy Department; on the lessons to be learned from the campaign: increase and strengthen surface forces.

59 Braybrook, Roy. BATTLE FOR THE FALKLANDS: III. AIR
FORCES. OSPREY MEN-AT-WAR series # 135. London: Osprey,
1982, 40 pp.
Included British and Argentine forces; one of a three-volume
series.

60 Bridge, T. D. "Time, Twis, Time Is Everything." ARMY
QUARTERLY AND DEFENCE JOURNAL, 112 (July 1982): 295–
304.
On the Falklands battle of 1914; allusion to the fact that two
British battlecruisers were rushed to the area and arrived just in
time to defeat the German squadron.

61 Brown, David. THE ROYAL NAVY AND THE FALKLANDS
WAR. Annapolis: NIP; London: Leo Cooper, 1987, 384 pp.
The best general survey of the naval phases of the campaign;
semi-official by the head of the Naval Historical Branch; useful maps and illustrations; no analysis or critique; submarine
operations remained secret; details on the task force deployment,
STUFT, attacks on RN ships from the air, and on ground operations.

62 Brown, James and Snyder, William P., eds. THE REGIONAL-
IZATION OF WARFARE: THE FALKLAND/MALVINAS IS-
LANDS, LEBANON, AND THE IRAN-IRAQ CONFLICT. New
Brunswick and Oxford: Transaction, 1985, 302 pp.
Papers presented at a conference, Dallas, Texas, April 1983,
reviewing three wars of 1982; Falklands/Malvinas, pp. 9–78, "The
Empire Strikes Back"; assessed Argentine forces: its air force was

aggressive and innovative, its navy was inactive, and its army was ineffective and demoralized; the British were praised for innovative logistical schemes and effective use of Harriers and helicopters.

63 Bruner, Ralph M. "Soviet Military Science and the Falklands Conflict." 3 Parts. NIProc, 111–112 (November 1985–January 1986): 90–95, 140–42, and 142–48.

Excerpts from Soviet professional armed forces journals; assessments of campaign maritime operations, logistics, and electronic warfare.

64 Bulmer-Thomas, Victor, ed. BRITAIN AND LATIN AMERICA: A CHANGING RELATIONSHIP. New York: Cambridge UP, 1989, 252 pp.

A series of papers; Anglo-Argentine relations "have fallen badly into disrepair," the wrong "signals" were sent, and there was forgetfulness about anniversaries; praise for the accounts of Charlton [91], Goebel [199], and Boyson [57].

65 Burden, Rodney A., et al. FALKLANDS: THE AIR WAR. New York: Sterling; London: Arms & Armour, 1986, 480 pp.

By the British Aviation Research Group; much detail on aircraft dispositions and operations; many colored pictures.

66 Burns, Jimmy. THE LAND THAT LOST ITS HEROES: THE FALKLANDS, THE POST-WAR AND ALFONSIN. London: Bloomsbury, 1987, 302 pp.

By the foreign correspondent of the FINANCIAL TIMES who remained in Argentina during the campaign and afterward; noted that Libya sent 20 Boeing 707s filled with arms to Argentina, SAS operations out of Chile, and the juxtaposition of war, World Cup soccer, and the papal visit; post-campaign purge of Junta and high-ranking officers, but interservice rivalry became more intense; trials of Junta led to sentences: Anaya = 14 years, Galtieri = 12 years, and Dozo = 8 years; a number of naive errors, e.g., calling Soviet Union and China Third World countries.

67 Burns, Robert Andrew. DIPLOMACY, WAR AND PARLIA-MENTARY DEMOCRACY: FURTHER LESSONS FROM THE

FALKLANDS OR ADVICE FROM ACADEME. CENTER FOR INTERNATIONAL AFFAIRS. New York: UP of America, 1985, 52 pp.

By a British diplomat; analysis and research as Fellow, Center for International Affairs, Harvard U.

68   Busser, Carlos. MALVINAS: LA GUENA INCONCLUSA. Buenos Aires: Ediciones Fernandez Reguera, 1987, 462 pp.

Included diplomatic preliminaries, day-by-day summary of operations of the campaign including an alleged attack on the INVINCIBLE, and the aftermath up to 1985.

69   Bustos, Dalmiro M. EL OTRO FRENTE DE LA GUERRA: LOS PADRES DE LAS MALVINAS. Buenos Aires: Ramos Americana Editora, 1982, 219 pp.

By a psychiatrist, father of a conscript, who set up a parents group and interviewed soldiers; included fascinating insights on the home front.

70   Buxton, Cindy and Price, Annie. SURVIVAL—SOUTH ATLANTIC. New York and London: Granada, 1983, 250 pp.

By journalists; excellent coverage; coined the term "Red Iceberg," describing HMS ENDURANCE.

71   Cable, Sir James. BRITAIN'S NAVAL FUTURE. Annapolis: NIP; London: Macmillan, 1982, 1983, 216 pp.

By statesman-diplomat-naval history observer; written after the 1981 Defence Review but before the Falklands/Malvinas campaign; "stop-press" note in the foreword; developed original concepts of naval strategy for the future.

72   Cable, Sir James. "Who Was Surprised in the Falklands and Why?: Prejudging and Inquiry." ENCOUNTER, 59 (September/October 1982): 39–42.

By an experienced diplomat and observer-statesman; contended that the Argentine invasion was predictable but not the time; the British reaction was not predictable; emphasis on the sovereignty issue.

73   Caillet-Bois, Ricardo R. UNA TIERRA ARGENTINA: LAS ISLAS MALVINAS. Buenos Aires: Peuser, 1948, 1949, 1982, 464 pp.

Like that of Goebel [199], this diplomatic review was favorable to Argentine claims; comprehensive and well-documented.

74 Calvert, Peter. THE FALKLANDS CRISIS: THE RIGHTS AND WRONGS. London: Pinter, 1982, 191 pp.

By a political science professor, U. Southampton; diplomatic review; noted the fundamental question was over sovereignty; a historical survey of the salient events of exploration and settlement.

75 Calvert, Peter. "Latin America and the United States during and after the Falklands Crisis." MILLENNIUM, 12 (Spring 1983): 69–78.

By an academic expert; reviewed the impact of the campaign on U.S.–Latin American relations.

76 Calvert, Peter. LATIN AMERICA IN THE TWENTIETH CENTURY. London: Macmillan, 1990, 248 pp.

Recent textbook by an academic expert.

77 Calvert, Peter. "Sovereignty and the Falklands Crisis." INTERNATIONAL AFFAIRS, 59 (Summer 1983): 405–14.

A review of the dispute as of the end of the campaign; still very much a live political issue and not resolved; conclusion: British claims by right of occupation seemed incontrovertible, but there was some question as to whether this claim was made.

78 Calvert, Susan and Calvert, Peter. ARGENTINA: POLITICAL CULTURE AND INSTABILITY. PITT LATIN AMERICAN series. Pittsburgh: U Pittsburgh P, 1989, 341 pp.

By a recent Ph.D.-holder and a professor, U. Southampton; review oriented around political and economic concepts; the campaign was not treated separately.

79 Calvert, Susan. "Political Culture and Political Stability in Argentina." Ph.D. diss., Southampton, n.d., 320 pp.

Ph.D. dissertation using academic analysis of Argentina based on social science models.

80 Campbell, Duncan and Rentoul, John. "The BELGRANO Cover-Up." NEW STATESMAN (31 August 1984): 8–10.

Reviewed aspects of the controversy in Great Britain over how, when, and where the BELGRANO was torpedoed; dispute over Rules of Engagement and changes to them; accusations of misinformation and that the government deceived Parliament; Clive Ponting [406] case noted.

81   Carballo, Pablo Marcos R. DIOS Y LOS HALCONES. Buenos Aires: Editorial Abril, 1982, 1983, 223 pp.

Semi-official account of the exploits of the Argentine pilots; overly-dramatic personal stories and colorful pictures of attacks on the frigate ARGONAUT, including a plane which hit her radio antenna; other realistic drawings of Super Etendard navy aircraft bombing INVINCIBLE depicting explosions and smoke emerging from several places below decks.

82   Cardoso, Oscar Raul, Kirschbaum, Ricardo, and Van der Kooy, Eduardo. FALKLANDS: THE SECRET PLOT. Buenos Aires: Sudamericana, 1983, 1987, 335 pp.

Translated by Bernard Ethell; Argentine journalists joined together to report on the campaign "to prevent the propaganda of the victor from becoming the official history of the vanquished" (p. iv); but, they claimed, as they investigated further, they discovered "a secret plot," a scheme worked out between General Galtieri and Vernon Walters involving formation of a South Atlantic Treaty Organization, Middle East peacekeeping, and intervention in Central America; called the Peruvian peace plan "Haig with a poncho!"; included the full text of the Galtieri-Reagan telephone conversation of 2 April (pp. 81–89); an unbalanced account with little on British actions and operations; sensationalist and narrow; poor translation.

83   Cardoso, Oscar Raul, Kirschbaum, Ricardo, and Van der Kooy, Eduardo. MALVINAS: LA TRAMA SECRETA. Buenos Aires: Sudamericana, 1983, 1984, 335 pp.

Spanish version of [82], the "secret plot" thesis; the 1984 publication designated as "11th edition"; praised by Jimmy Burns [66] as well-researched and least biased of the Argentine accounts.

84   Carr, Jean. ANOTHER STORY: WOMEN AND THE FALKLANDS WAR. London: Hamilton, 1984, 179 pp.

By a SUNDAY MIRROR journalist who investigated problems through numerous interviews; from the perspective of the families of British servicemen; "the reverse side of the Falklands coin" contrasted the "glamourised public view against the tragic human aftermath" (p. vii); experiences of trauma associated with the soldiers and their families; compensation for the wounded was inadequate; the South Atlantic Fund of 16 million pounds was to supplement but its mismanagement led to depletion of that source.

85   Carril, Bonifacio del. THE MALVINAS/FALKLANDS CASE. Buenos Aires: CIGA, 1982, 85 pp.

By the former foreign minister of Argentina; proposed solution (as of 23 April 1982); reviewed events of the eighteenth and nineteenth centuries; original possession was rightly Argentine; Britain had not complied with the U.N. Resolution of 1965.

86   Carrington, Lord Peter. REFLECT ON THINGS PAST: THE MEMOIRS OF LORD CARRINGTON. London: Collins; New York: Harper & Row: 1988, 1989, 416 pp.

Memoirs of the foreign secretary of Great Britain at the time of the invasion; he resigned over the crisis; Falklands/Malvinas events and alliance, pp. 348–96; described his views and events as they affected British foreign policy and him as foreign secretary.

87   Catterall, Peter, ed. BRITISH HISTORY, 1945–1987: AN ANNOTATED BIBLIOGRAPHY. Cambridge, MA and Oxford: Blackwell, 1990, 875 pp.

A general bibliography on post-war British history; 15,000 entries; extensive and timely.

88   Cawkell, Mary B. R., Maling, D. H., and Cawkell, E. M. THE FALKLAND ISLANDS. New York: St. Martins; London: Macmillan, 1960, 1961, 252 pp.

Comprehensive; on exploration, settlements, geological structure, climate, and the natural life of plants and birds.

89   Cawkell, Mary B. R. THE FALKLANDS STORY, 1592–1982. Shropshire: Anthony Nelson, 1983, 90 pp.

Foreword by E. W. Hunter Christie; updated chronological and natural history.

90   Ceron, Sergio. MALVINAS: ¿GESTA HEROICA O DERROTA VERGONZOSA? Buenos Aires: Sudamericana, 1984, 344 pp.

A popular Argentine account in paperback.

91 Charlton, Michael. THE LITTLE PLATOON: DIPLOMACY AND THE FALKLANDS DISPUTE. Oxford: Blackwell, 1989, 244 pp.

From eight broadcasts on BBC Radio Three, summer 1987; a series of oral interviews with prominent British, Argentines, and Americans to explore the background and history of the dispute; noted the "totally uncompromising lobby"; made events more understandable.

92 Chesneau, Roger. AIRCRAFT CARRIERS OF THE WORLD: 1914 TO THE PRESENT: AN ILLUSTRATED ENCYCLOPEDIA. Annapolis: NIP, 1984, 288 pp.

Catalogue of all aircraft carriers of the world; detailed schematics and information on capabilities and alterations.

93 Chippindale, Peter and Horrie, Chris. STICK IT UP YOUR PUNTER!: THE RISE AND FALL OF THE "SUN." London: Heinemann, 1990, 372 pp.

Reviewed the machinations of the most sensational newspaper which was adept at manufacturing news, the authors claimed, e.g., reporting "invasion" days before it occurred, but the falsification was seemingly forgotten when it actually took place; recalled GOTCHA! headline.

94 Churchill, Winston S. THE WORLD CRISIS. 6 vols. (also 4-, 2-, and 1-vol. eds.). New York: Scribners, 1923–1931, 1939, 1951, 1960, 1963, various (6 vols., 2800 pp.; 4 vols., 1800 pp.; 2 vols., 1200 pp.; 1 vol., 866 pp.).

Coverage of battle of Falklands while Churchill was first lord of the Admiralty.

95 Clarke, Harold D., Mishler, William, and Whiteley, Paul. "William Mishler and Paul Whiteley Recapturing the Falklands: Models of Conservative Popularity, 1979–1983." BRITISH JOURNAL OF POLITICAL SCIENCE, 20 (January 1990): 63–81.

Response to D. Sanders, et al. [443]; claimed their statistical procedures were misleading; reanalysis of the model; Sanders claimed the campaign exerted inconsequential influence on the Conservative popularity; other variables failed to eliminate the Falklands effect.

96 Coleridge, Samuel Taylor. THE ANCIENT MARINER or THE RIME OF THE ANCIENT MARINER. Boston: Heath, 1798, 1897, 1911, 94 pp.
A famous lyrical ballad describing a location in the South Atlantic.

97 Coll, Alberto R. and Arend, Anthony C., eds. THE FALK-LANDS WAR: LESSONS FOR STRATEGY, DIPLOMACY AND INTERNATIONAL LAW. Boston and London: Allen & Unwin, 1985, 252 pp.
A collection of 15 papers from a conference, University of Virginia law school, fall of 1982; participants included scholars and international lawyers; one expert noted that the antagonists observed the laws of war more closely than in any conflict since World War II; other papers on U.N., OAS, and boundary disputes; some authors were obviously not informed on Falklands/Malvinas issues.

98 Colledge, James J. THE SHIPS OF THE ROYAL NAVY: AN HISTORICAL INDEX. 2 vols. Newton Abbot: David & Charles; Annapolis: NIP, 1969, 1987, 1988, 1989, 500 pp.
A comprehensive reference source; 14,000 entries; details on every British and Commonwealth warship since the 15th century; data, not illustrations.

99 Collier, Simon. "The First Falklands War? Argentine Atti-tudes." INTERNATIONAL AFFAIRS, 59 (Summer 1983): 459–64.
Review article on six works from Argentina; Argentines were surprised at the invasion; some wild explanations on why the British responded: Britain in the process of decolonization, oil, etc.

100 Colombo, Jorge Luis. " 'Super Etendard' Naval Aircraft Op-erations during the Malvinas War." NWCR, 37 (May 1984): 12–22.
By commanding officer, naval aviation squadron of Super Etendards; recalled initiatives in training and installing EXOCETs without French assistance; attack on INVINCIBLE on 30 May was joint air force/naval effort with six aircraft; observers saw smoke; recalled other attacks on SHEFFIELD and ATLANTIC CONVEYOR.

101 COMBAT FLEETS OF THE WORLD: THEIR SHIPS, AIR-CRAFT, AND ARMAMENT. French original: FLOTTES DE COMBAT. Annapolis: NIP, various annual editions, c. 900 pp.

Edited by Jean L. Couhat; French publication; a standard reference source with detailed information on "entire naval programmes" of 160 nations; 3700 illustrations.

102 Committee for Economic Development. ECONOMIC DEVELOPMENT ISSUES: LATIN AMERICA. Supplementary Paper # 21. New York: CED, 1967, 342 pp.

Series of essays; Roberto Alemann, "Economic Development of Argentina," pp. 1–59, on Peronist period, 1945–1964.

103 Connell-Smith, Gordon. "The OAS and the Falklands Conflict." THE WORLD TODAY, 38 (September 1982): 340–47.

A diplomatic survey of the role of the OAS, which tilted for Argentina.

104 Conway's. CONWAY'S ALL THE WORLD'S FIGHTING SHIPS, 1947–1982. 2 vols. Annapolis: NIP, 1983, 570 pp.

Edited by Robert Gardiner; reference source with historical focus; Falklands/Malvinas campaign, pp. 128–29; noted assembling the British task force "was a masterpiece of speed and efficiency" (p. 128); the Argentine navy was unprepared.

105 Coote, John O. " 'Send Her Victorious . . . ' " NIProc, 109 (January 1983): 35–42.

By former naval officer turned journalist; reviewed British naval operations and logistical provisions; "brilliant improvisation"; no AEW capability; the British must have lamented the lack of attack carriers such as old VICTORIOUS.

106 Cordesman, Anthony H. "The Falklands Crisis: Emerging Lessons for Power Projection and Force Planning." ARMED FORCES JOURNAL, 120 (September 1982): 29–46.

By prominent defense expert; corrected "myths" such as erroneous claim that aluminum hulls burned; only the Argentine air force proved to be formidable; its army conduct was "peculiar."

107 Cordesman, Anthony H. and Wagner, Abraham R. THE LESSONS OF MODERN WAR. 3 vols. Boulder, CO: Westview, 1990, 1618 pp.

Ambitious effort to review four conflicts including the Falklands/Malvinas campaign; much detail, poor maps.

108 Cosgrave, Patrick. CARRINGTON: A LIFE AND A POLICY. London: Dent, 1985, 192 pp.
Biography of the foreign secretary; section on "the Fall," pp. 16–41, and "Defence of the Realm," pp. 86–112.

109 Cosgrave, Patrick. THATCHER: THE FIRST. London: Bodley Head, 1985, 252 pp.
Biography, emphasizing the heated struggle for leadership; on the campaign, pp. 179–224.

110 Craig, Christopher. "Fighting by the Rules." NWCR, 37 (May 1984): 23–27.
Details on Rules of Engagement and Exclusion Zones, aspects of the international law of war; an emotive issue related to the controversy over the BELGRANO sinking.

111 Critchley, Mike, ed. FALKLANDS TASK FORCE PORTFOLIO. 2 parts. Liskeard: Maritime, 1982, 232 pp.
Magazine format, many illustrations; published at the end of the campaign.

112 Curteis, Ian. THE FALKLANDS PLAY: A TELEVISION PLAY. London: Hutchinson, 1987, 192 pp.
Author was commissioned by BBC-1 to write this play, not a documentary, on the campaign; had previously done a three-hour play on Suez; incorporated "Haigspeak" and drunkenness of Galtieri; argued that the British intervention was inevitable and right; but play cancelled and never televised.

113 Dabat, Alejandro and Lorenzano, Luis. ARGENTINA: THE MALVINAS AND THE END OF MILITARY RULE. London: Verso, 1982, 1984, 205 pp.
Translated by Ralph Johnstone; by Argentine socialists; campaign divided the Left in Argentina but both sides agreed with Argentine claims and condemnation of British colonialism.

114 Dabat, Alejandro and Lorenzano, Luis. CONFLICTO MALVINENSE Y CRISIS NACIONAL. Buenos Aires: Teoria y Politica, 1982, 286 pp.

Argentine socialists reviewed the campaign and afterward.

115   Dalyell, Tam. MISRULE: HOW MRS. THATCHER HAS MISLED PARLIAMENT FROM THE SINKING OF THE "BELGRANO" TO THE WRIGHT AFFAIR. London: Hamilton, 1987, 176 pp.

By the radical MP, the most outspoken opponent of the campaign; suspended from Parliament in 1982 and 1986 for personal verbal attacks on Thatcher: "a bounder, a liar, a deceiver."

116   Dalyell, Tam. ONE MAN'S FALKLANDS. London: Woolf, 1982, 144 pp.

By radical MP; attacked Falklands/Malvinas campaign on moral grounds, "an act of naked aggression"; sinking of BELGRANO was ruthless, unnecessary, and bloodthirsty.

117   Dalyell, Tam. THATCHER'S TORPEDO: THE SINKING OF THE "BELGRANO." London: Woolf, 1983, 80 pp.

Introduction by Paul Rogers; by the radical MP who claimed the British government welcomed the opportunity to attack Argentina as a political diversion from domestic difficulties.

118   Daoudi, M. S. and Dajani, M. S. "Sanctions: The Falklands Episode." WORLD TODAY, 39 (April 1983): 150–60.

On the sanctions implemented by the British, Argentina, and the European Community.

119   Dar, E. H. "Strategy in the Falklands War." NIProc, 109 (March 1983): 132–34.

By general, Pakistani army; Argentina obstinately decided to invade; the British had few effective options but retaliation; Argentina failed to properly oppose the British landing, no plan of defense; nevertheless, British action was "sluggish."

120   Dartford, Mark, ed. FALKLANDS AFTERMATH: FORCES '85. London: Marshall Cavendish, 1984, 144 pp.

Large picture book; wide ranging topics, too much so.

121   Dartford, Mark, ed. FALKLANDS ARMOURY. New York: Sterling; Poole: Blandford, 1985, 104 pp.

On weapons and equipment; many detailed illustrations.

122 Davis, Peter G. "SBS: The History that Can Be Told." AQDJ, 114 (July 1984): 302–08.
By lieutenant colonel, Royal Marines; on Special Boat Service; usually operated in secrecy.

123 Dawson, Philip S. BRITISH SUPERLINERS OF THE SIXTIES: A DESIGN APPRECIATION OF THE "ORIANA," "CANBERRA" AND "QE2." London: Conway, 1990, 154 pp.
Details on the actual design of these liners and rationales for those particular lay-outs; two of these liners participated in STUFT.

124 De Arcangelis, Mario. ELECTRONIC WARFARE: FROM THE BATTLE OF TSUSHIMA TO THE FALKLANDS AND LEBANON CONFLICTS. New York: Sterling; Poole: Blandford, 1985, 320 pp.
On exotic innovations during the century.

125 DEFENCE. A monthly journal. Redhill, Surrey.
Devoted a special issue, November 1982, to the campaign.

126 Defoe, Daniel. ROBINSON CRUSOE. New York: Sears, 1719, 1948, 246 pp.
Classic fiction modelled on the adventures of Alexander Selkirk, a Scottish sailor forced to live on an isolated island which could have been the Falklands/Malvinas.

127 Destefani, Laurio H. MALVINAS, GEORGIAS Y SANDWICH DEL SUR ANTE EL CONFLICTO CON GRAN BRETANA. Buenos Aires: Edipress, 1982, 143 pp.
By retired admiral; "The Malvinas are Argentine," inherited from Spain, and never to be given up!

128 Destefani, Laurio H. THE MALVINAS, THE SOUTH GEORGIAS AND THE SOUTH SANDWICH ISLANDS: CONFLICT WITH GREAT BRITAIN. Buenos Aires: Edipress, 1982, 143 pp.
Translated version of [127].

129 Dillon, George Michael. THE FALKLANDS: POLITICS AND WAR. New York: St. Martins, 1988, 280 pp.
By U. Lancaster academic; an excellent detailed review of British actions and inactions in the decades before 1982; the

primary issue was sovereignty but the islanders refused to agree to negotiate that issue; the sovereignty dispute degenerated into military confrontation; the British decision to expel the Argentines exposed fundamental weaknesses at the center of British decision-making; a detailed discussion of the BELGRANO episode and cabinet decisions; the "Falklands factor" boosted Thatcher from the worst to the most favored prime minister in British history, virtually overnight, he claimed.

130   Disciullo, Alfredo R.F. MALVINAS 1983: ARGENTINA CONTRAATACHAI! n.p.: n.d., 130 pp.
A popular Argentine account of the aftermath.

131   Dobson, Christopher, Miller, John, and Payne, Ronald. THE FALKLANDS CONFLICT. London: Hodder & Stoughton, 1982, 223 pp.
By journalists; an example of the "rush-to-publication" phenomenon; a conventional account.

132   Dockrill, Michael L. BRITISH DEFENCE SINCE 1945. New York and Oxford: Blackwell, 1988, 178 pp.
By U. London academic; reviewed the development of defense policy, especially at the times of key events: Korean, Suez, and Falklands/Malvinas campaigns; 1957 and 1981 defense reviews.

133   Doxey, Margaret. "International Sanctions: Trials of Strength or Tests of Weakness?" MILLENNIUM, 12 (Spring 1983): 79–87.
Article on the efforts short of war.

134   Dunnett, Denzil. "Self-determination and the Falklands." INTERNATIONAL AFFAIRS, 59 (Summer 1983): 415–28.
"Let the people decide," insisted Thatcher, yet Kelpers were not really considered a "people"; self-determination was the issue.

135   Dyson, Tony. HMS "HERMES," 1959–1984: A PICTORIAL HISTORY. Liskeard: Maritime, 1984, 160 pp.
Flagship of the task force; evolved from strike carrier to anti-submarine warfare (ASW) to helicopter to Harrier carrier.

136 . THE ECONOMIST. A weekly newsmagazine. London.
Consistent coverage of the campaign.

137 Eddy, Paul, Linklater, Magnus, and Gillman, Peter, eds. THE FALKLANDS WAR. SUNDAY TIMES INSIGHT TEAM. London: Deutsch, 1982, 286 pp.
By 24 journalists; written in September 1982 and the first book on the campaign; little time for reflection; reviewed the 74 days.

138 Edmonds, Martin, ed. THE DEFENCE EQUATION: BRITISH MILITARY SYSTEMS, POLICY PLANNING AND PERFORMANCE. London: Brassey's, 1986, 250 pp.
11 essays presenting detailed background on British defense problems; the campaign afforded a "magnificent opportunity" to demonstrate the continued utility of RN forces.

139 Eltzer, Bernardo A. LA ARMADA ARGENTINA Y EL MANEJO DE LA OPINION PUBLICA EN LOS DIAS PREVOIS AL CONFLICTO MALVINAS: BIBLIOGRAFIA COMENTADA. Buenos Aires: Ediciones, 1987, 84 pp.
A bibliographical index.

140 English, Adrian and Watts, Anthony. BATTLE FOR THE FALKLANDS: II. NAVAL FORCES. OSPREY MEN-AT-ARMS series # 134. London: Osprey, 1982, 40 pp.
One of the Osprey series.

141 "The Englishwoman's Wardrobe." BBC-TV Documentary, 20 November 1986.
Interview with Thatcher; she revealed her "most cherished dress" story, a navy blue one which, she said, sustained her through the campaign.

142 Estival, B. and Guillot, J. L'EXTRAORDINAIRE ADVENTURE DE L'EXOCET. Paris: Editions de la Cite, 1988.
Story of the international EXOCET missile, its development, use, and anecdotes.

143 Ethell, Jeffrey and Price, Alfred. AIR WAR SOUTH ATLANTIC. London: Sidgwick & Jackson, 1983, 1984, 260 pp.
Able to use sources from all British and Argentine services; concluded that the British air victory was due to air-to-air refuelling capabilities and Harriers; the story of the Argentine Super Etendard attack jets; there were five, but one was used for spares;

the Argentines were plagued by technical defects, especially bomb fuzzes, many of which were of British manufacture!

144   Ethell, Jeffrey and Price, Alfred. GUERRA AEREA SUDAT-LANTICA. Buenos Aires: n.p., 1987, 260 pp.
Translation of [143].

145   THE FALKLAND ISLANDS: THE FACTS. London: HMSO, 1982.
Fact pamphlet published by the government.

146   FALKLAND ISLANDS GAZETTE. Stanley.
Vol. I of January 1891; an example of older media; source for local history and domestic developments.

147   FALKLAND ISLANDS JOURNAL. Stanley, recent, various.
Newer media; articles on exploration, Antarctica, wildlife, commercial sea activities, and a royal visit of 1973.

148   "Falkland Sound/Voces de Malvinas." A play.
Performed at Royal Theatre, London, summer 1983.

149   "The Falklands Operation." Supplement to ARMED FORCES MAGAZINE. London: Allan and RUSI, n.d.
Photographic record available from RUSI, presumably immediately after the campaign, at 85 pence.

150   "Falkland Postscripts." NIProc, 109 (June 1983): 99–124.
A series of "afterthoughts"; short articles by J. Goldrick, R. Scheina, A. Baker, and S. Morison; Goldrick noted that British strategic doctrine was "gravely flawed" prior to the campaign.

151   "Falklands: Task Force South." Video. Tinley Park, IL: Fusion, n.d., 120 min.
By the BBC camera team during the 10–week campaign; most footage from the British flagship.

152   Feldman, David L. "Argentina, 1945–1971: Military Assistance, Military Spending, and the Political Activity of the Armed Forces." JOURNAL OF INTERAMERICAN STUDIES AND WORLD AFFAIRS, 24 (August 1982): 321–36.
By academic from West Virginia State; correlation and dilemma of military assistance and military intervention.

153 Ferns, Henry Stanley. ARGENTINA. NATIONS OF THE MODERN WORLD series. New York: Praeger; London: Ernest Brown, 1969, 284 pp.
From a standard series of textbooks; general history; good for background.

154 Ferns, Henry Stanley. BRITAIN AND ARGENTINA IN THE NINETEENTH CENTURY. Oxford: Clarendon; New York: Arno, 1960, 1970, 1977, 527 pp.
Establishment of British interests and later problems, e.g., loans, religion, Falklands/Malvinas; dramatic expansion of British capital investment.

155 Flayhart, William H. and Warwick, Ronald W. " 'The Liner She's a Lady.' " NIProc, 110 (November 1984): 53–64.
By chief officer, QE2; quote from Kipling; QE2 was requisitioned for service 4 May through 11 June.

156 Flintham, Victor. AIR WARS AND AIRCRAFT: A DETAILED RECORD OF AIR COMBAT, 1945 TO THE PRESENT. New York: Facts on File, 1990, 415 pp.
100 maps, 200 illustrations; descriptions of wars and crises; Falklands/Malvinas campaign, pp. 370–80.

157 Fogwill, Rodolfo Enrique. LOS PICHY–CYEGOS: VISIONES DE UNA BATALLA SUBTERRANEA [VISIONS OF THE SUBTERRANEAN BATTLE]. Buenos Aires: Ediciones de la Flor, 1983, 135 pp.
Original Argentine satire on the campaign.

158 Foot, Paul. "How the Peace Was Torpedoed." NEW STATESMAN (13 May 1983): 8–10.
On the BELGRANO sinking, ordered by Thatcher, which "scuppered" a possible peace settlement; John Nott's claim that BELGRANO was "closing on the task force" was not true.

159 Fordham, Angela. FALKLAND ISLANDS: A BIBLIOGRAPHY OF 50 EXAMPLES OF PRINTED MAPS BEARING SPECIFIC REFERENCE. MAP COLLECTORS' series # 11. London: Map Collectors, 1964, 18 pp.
Bibliography restricted to maps of islands.

160　Foster, Nigel. MAKING OF A ROYAL MARINE COMMANDO. Novato, CA: Presidio, 1990, 190 pp.
Preface by General Julian Thompson; illustrated variety of roles throughout the world.

161　Foulkes, Haroldo. LOS KELPERS EN LAS MALVINAS Y EN LA PATAGONIA. Buenos Aires: Corregidor, 1983, 139 pp.
Argentine account on the Kelpers.

162　Foulkes, Haroldo. MALVINAS: 74 DIAS ALUCINANTES EN PUERTO ARGENTINO. Buenos Aires: Corregidor, 1984, 188 pp.
Recounted the days of the campaign at Port Stanley.

163　Foulkes, Haroldo. LAS MALVINAS: UNA CAUSA NACIONAL. Buenos Aires: Corregidor, 1978, 1982, 165 pp.
Details on background, the economy, Falkland Islands Company, oil, and Shackleton survey, SHACKLETON I [452].

164　Fowler, William. THE BATTLE FOR THE FALKLANDS: I. LAND FORCES. OSPREY MEN-AT-ARMS series # 133. London: Osprey, 1982, 40 pp.
From Osprey series.

165　Fox, Robert. ANTARCTICA AND THE SOUTH ATLANTIC: DISCOVERY, DEVELOPMENT, AND DISPUTE. London: BBC, 1985, 336 pp.
Details on Falklands/Malvinas policy after the campaign; Fox, a BBC journalist, returned in December 1982; observations of the details of the planned "Fortress Falklands"; returned yet again in 1984 and joined ENDURANCE for ice patrol duty and exploration.

166　Fox, Robert. EYEWITNESS FALKLANDS: A PERSONAL ACCOUNT OF THE FALKLANDS CAMPAIGN. London: Methuen, 1982, 350 pp.
By BBC Radio journalist; his personal observations; he was the only journalist to receive an MBE award; especially good on the land campaign.

167　Fraga, Jorge A. LA ARGENTINA Y EL ATLANTICO SUR: CONFLICTOS Y OBJECTIVOS. Buenos Aires: Pleamar, 1983, 340 pp.

By chairman, Islas Malvinas Institute, a quasi-military agency, January 1982; called for an end of the endless round of negotiations.

168 Franks, Lord Joseph. FALKLAND ISLANDS REVIEW: REPORT OF A COMMITTEE OF PRIVY COUNSELLORS. Cmnd 8787. London: HMSO, 1983.

The FRANKS REPORT; the premier study of British actions and inaction prior to the Argentine invasion; chaired by a distinguished academic-diplomat; one of the best sources on the diplomatic background; concluded that the Thatcher government was not responsible for the Argentine invasion, but a point-by-point indictment of the government action and inaction; there was no organized dissent to the conclusions.

169 Freedman, Lawrence. "The Atlantic Crisis." INTERNATIONAL AFFAIRS, 58 (Summer 1982): 395–412.

From Chatham House research project; about NATO, economic malaise, and deteriorating strategic alliance.

170 Freedman, Lawrence. "Bridgehead Revisited: The Literature of the Falklands." INTERNATIONAL AFFAIRS, 59 (Summer 1983): 445–52.

By U. London academic; review essay which surveyed some opponents of the campaign: e.g., Tam Dalyell [116] and Anthony Barnett [21]; on government-media relations.

171 Freedman, Lawrence. BRITAIN AND THE FALKLANDS WAR. MAKING CONTEMPORARY BRITAIN series. Oxford: Blackwell, 1988, 139 pp.

Aimed at undergraduates; surveyed government-media relations; comprehensive coverage.

172 Freedman, Lawrence. "British Defence Policy after the Falklands." WORLD TODAY, 38 (September 1982): 331–39.

Lessons on defense policy after the campaign; revisionist case.

173 Freedman, Lawrence. "The Falklands War of 1982." FOREIGN AFFAIRS, 61 (Fall 1982): 196–210.

An early example of academic, scholarly coverage of outstanding quality; the campaign was a classic case study of limited war; concluded Argentine EXOCETs were only partially successful because the cumbersome British countermeasures were effective; the British failed in media relations; noted "comic opera" saga of scrap metal merchants.

174 Freedman, Lawrence. "Intelligence Operations in the Falklands." INTELLIGENCE AND NATIONAL SECURITY, 1 (September 1986): 309–35.

By prestigious academic expert who reviewed intelligence factors from the British perspective; the campaign attracted extraordinary international attention; the FRANKS REPORT [168] focused on intelligence and the failure of warnings; role of attaches in Latin America had been redirected toward arms sales; HMS ENDURANCE and the Americans provided SIGINT; much early intelligence from Portsmouth and Plymouth public libraries!; the most serious intelligence error was at Goose Green when the Argentine force was estimated at 400 when there were 1100 there; could have been a disaster at an especially crucial moment.

175 Freedman, Lawrence and Gamba-Stonehouse, Virginia. SIGNALS OF WAR: THE FALKLANDS CONFLICT OF 1982. Boston and London: Faber & Faber, 1990, 512 pp.

By prominent and widely acclaimed academics from both perspectives; perhaps the best, most comprehensive, considered account of the background, diplomacy, or lack of it, and geopolitics leading to and during the campaign; noted "the inclement and inhospitable Islands themselves never became a jewel in the British imperial crown"; they immediately disposed of the conspiracy theory concerning BELGRANO: the attack was for purely military reasons; revisionist view on Argentine Junta: Anaya previously seen as more aggressive and insistent but recent evidence pointed to common and joint responsibility of all three; details on Haig shuttle diplomacy, Peruvian peace plan, and efforts of the U.N.

176 Friedman, Norman. BRITISH CARRIER AVIATION: THE EVOLUTION OF THE SHIPS AND THEIR AIRCRAFT. Annapolis: NIP, 1988, 384 pp.

By noted military expert; from seaplane carriers to carriers of Falklands/Malvinas campaign; 400 illustrations; recounted the unique British contributions to carrier aviation.

177 Friedman, Norman. "The Falklands War: Lessons Learned and Mislearned." ORBIS, 26 (Winter 1983): 907–40.
Lengthy article of assessment; focused on the lessons to be learned by the U.S.; for Argentina, the lack of interservice cooperation was fatal, the performance of its army officers being most deplorable; good and bad aspects of British handling of the media.

178 Frost, John. 2 PARA FALKLANDS: THE BATTALION AT WAR. London: Sphere, 1983, 1984, 192 pp.
Story of soldiers written by soldiers; British participants of the land war.

179 Fuchs, Sir Vivian. OF ICE AND MEN: THE STORY OF THE BRITISH ANTARCTIC SURVEY, 1943–1973. Oswestry: Nelson, 1982, 383 pp.
These operations began as naval efforts associated with World War II and evolved into scientific endeavors; details on the survey in narrative form.

180 Fursdon, Edward. THE FALKLANDS AFTERMATH: PICKING UP THE PIECES. London: Leo Cooper, 1988, 219 pp.
By defense correspondent, DAILY TELEGRAPH, who visited after the campaign; recounted post-war developments of "Fortress Falklands"; building of the new, expanded airfield at a cost of 350 million pounds; details on "cleaning up" and rehabilitation.

181 Gamba-Stonehouse, Virginia. LA CUESTION Y LA CRISIS. Buenos Aires, 1983.
A review of the issues and problems of the crisis.

182 Gamba-Stonehouse, Virginia. THE FALKLANDS/MALVINAS WAR: MODEL FOR NORTH-SOUTH CRISIS PREVENTION. Boston: Allen & Unwin, 1987, 224 pp.
By expert from Argentine perspective; a unique approach of study, as a model for North-South relationships focusing on the roles of the U.S. and Latin America; concluded that there was a need for more effective communications between the differing spheres.

183 Gamba-Stonehouse, Virginia. MALVINAS: CONFIDEN-

CIAL Buenos Aires: Publinter, 1982, 40 pp.
A pamphlet which assessed the crisis.

184 Gamba-Stonehouse, Virginia. EL PEON DE LA REINA. Buenos Aires: Sudamericana, 1984, 207 pp.
On the crisis of 1982 concerning the Falklands/Malvinas, Georgias, and Sandwich islands.

185 Gamba-Stonehouse, Virginia. THE SOUTH ATLANTIC CONFLICT: AN ARGENTINE VIEW. Buenos Aires: Grafica Particios, 1982.
By an expert from the Argentine perspective.

186 Gamba-Stonehouse, Virginia. STRATEGY IN THE SOUTHERN OCEANS: A SOUTH AMERICAN VIEW. London: Pinter, 1989, 155 pp.
By noted scholar observing strategic, especially naval, factors of the Falklands/Malvinas campaign; addressed the maritime dimension of international security, considering revived British interests and the concerns of Argentina, Brazil, and others with interests in the South Atlantic.

187 Gambini, Hugo. CRONICA DOCUMENTAL DE LAS MALVINAS. 3 vols. Buenos Aires: Biblioteca de Redaccion, 1982, 1160 pp.
Many documents and illustrations in this comprehensive, multi-volume compilation of the history of the dispute and the campaign.

188 Gandia, Enrique de. "Las Islas Argentinas de San Antonio." REVISTA GEOGRAFICA ARGENTINA, 24 (1945): 265–70.
A thesis that Duarte Barbosa discovered the islands.

189 Gardner, John. WIN, LOSE OR DIE. New York: Putnams, 1989, 319 pp.
Gardner has revived Ian Fleming's master spy James Bond, who in this spy novel recalled secret service in the Falklands/Malvinas operations.

190 Garrison, Peter. "CV": CARRIER AVIATION. PRESIDIO AIR POWER series. Novato, CA: Presidio; London: Arms & Armour, 1980, 1984, 1988, 110 pp.

Up-to-date coverage of the topic including the Falklands/Malvinas campaign and the latest American attack carriers.

191 Gavshon, Arthur L. and Rice, Desmond. EL HUNDIMIENTO DEL "BELGRANO." Buenos Aires: Emece Editores, 1984, 234 pp.
Spanish translation of [192].

192 Gavshon, Arthur L. and Rice, Desmond. THE SINKING OF THE "BELGRANO." London: Secker & Warburg; Sevenoaks: New England, 1984, 254 pp.
Both were published authors but not on subjects related to this one; the most detailed account from the conspiracy thesis position; disputed by Hastings and Jenkins [225], among others; "the Tam Dalyell line"; no attempt to verify claims.

193 Gelb, Norman. "Thatcher's Victory: The Falklands Factor." NEW LEADER, 65 (12–26 July 1982): 5–6.
Claimed it transformed the face of British politics and the momentum of opponents was destroyed; only the far Left opposed.

194 Geraghty, Tony. WHO DARES WINS: INSIDE THE SPECIAL AIR SERVICE. 2nd ed. subtitle: THE SPECIAL AIR SERVICE, 1950 TO THE FALKLANDS. Nashville: Battery; London: Arms & Armour, 1980, 1981, 1983, 320 pp.
Rare history of a force which operated in secrecy; second edition included Falklands/Malvinas campaign, pp. 218–86.

195 Gething, Michael J. MILITARY HELICOPTERS. WARBIRDS ILLUSTRATED series # 13. London: Arms & Armour, 1983, 65 pp.
"Military buff-type" history of operations of rotary-wing aircraft.

196 GLOBE AND LAUREL. JOURNAL OF THE ROYAL MARINES. Southsea, since 1892.
An "in-house" journal; several articles presenting first-hand accounts of the campaign.

197 Godden, John, ed. HARRIER: SKI JUMP TO VICTORY. Washington and London: Brassey's, 1983, 141 pp.
Foreword by Admiral Lord Lewin; 100 illustrations; specifically about the Falklands/Malvinas campaign and the vital role of

Harriers; use of 28 RN and 14 RAF Harriers; personal accounts of pilots.

198 Goebel, Julius. LA PUGNA POR LAS ISLAS MALVINAS: UN ESTUDIO DE LA HISTORIA LEGAL Y DIPLOMATICA. Buenos Aires: Abaco, 1927, 1950, 522 pp.
Spanish translation of [199].

199 Goebel, Julius. THE STRUGGLE FOR THE FALKLAND ISLANDS: A STUDY IN LEGAL AND DIPLOMATIC HISTORY. New Haven and London: Yale UP, 1927, 1982, 512 pp.
New foreword by J.C.J. Metford; original edition written under conditions of U.S. isolationism during early interwar period by an international lawyer of Yale Law School; referred to undocumented "secret agreement" in chapter 7, pp. 316–63; noted Peron and his followers "played up xenophobic passions of the masses"; scholarly position most favorable to Argentine view; Spanish edition [198] and Yale reprint during crisis; Calvert [74] claimed international law irrelevant in this case.

200 Goldblat, Jozef and Millan, Victor. THE FALKLANDS/MALVINAS CONFLICT. Solna, Sweden: Stockholm International Peace Research, 1983, 70 pp.
Sponsored by an international think-tank; concerned that the conflict greatly stimulated the arms race and continued the arms build-up; conflict has meant delay to political settlement, creating more problems and tensions.

201 Goodman, Edward Julius. THE EXPLORATION OF SOUTH AMERICA: AN ANNOTATED BIBLIOGRAPHY. THEMES IN EUROPEAN EXPANSION series #4. New York: Garland, 1983, 194 pp.
919 entries, 6 of which were under "Malvinas."

202 Goodman, Edward Julius. THE EXPLORERS OF SOUTH AMERICA. New York: Macmillan; London: Collier, 1972, 416 pp.
Included discovery and settlement of Falkland/Malvinas Islands.

203 Gould, Diana. ON THE SPOT: THE SINKING OF THE "BELGRANO." London: Woolf, 1984, 80 pp.

Introduced by Tam Dalyell; Gould became a kind of "pop-hero" when she, a Gloucestershire housewife, questioned Thatcher about the sinking of BELGRANO; dubbed "a prodigious West Country battle-axe" and "Tam Dalyell in drag."

204 Graham-Yooll, Andrew. A STATE OF FEAR: MEMORIES OF ARGENTINA'S NIGHTMARE. New York: Hippocrene; London: Eland, 1986, 180 pp.
By Argentine writer, an opponent of the invasion; focused on political murders of the regime.

205 Grant, Bernhard S. H. THE POSTAGE STAMPS OF THE FALKLAND ISLANDS AND DEPENDENCIES. London: Gibbons, 1952, 140 pp.
Details about a unique feature of Falklands activities, the basis for some international renown.

206 Greenberg, Susan. REJOICE!: MEDIA FREEDOM AND THE FALKLANDS. London: Campaign for Press and Broadcasting Freedom, 1983.
A study of media-government relationships during the campaign.

207 Greenway, Mary E. THE GEOLOGY OF THE FALKLAND ISLANDS. London: British Antarctic Survey, 1972, 48 pp.
One of a series of scientific reports of the British Antarctic Survey.

208 Grove, Eric J. "After the Falklands." NIProc, 112 (March 1986): 121-29.
Described the revitalized RN, the campaign having saved it from some of the proposed cuts of 1981; detailed changes and alterations; White Paper of 1985 called for level spending, personnel in the RN to be reduced from 62,000 to 51,000.

209 Grove, Eric J. THE FUTURE OF SEA POWER. Annapolis: NIP; London: Routledge, 1990, 293 pp.
Foreword by Admiral Sir Julian Oswald; a much-acclaimed analysis of maritime strategic thinking; compared with Mahan and Corbett; frequent references to incidents and lessons learned

from the Falklands/Malvinas campaign; concluded with a typology for navies, ranking "global forces" as follows: Rank 1: U.S., U.S.S.R., Great Britain, France, . . . and under Rank 4. Medium Regional Force, Argentina, . . . etc., to Rank 9.

210   Grove, Eric J. VANGUARD TO TRIDENT: BRITISH NAVAL POWER SINCE WORLD WAR II. Annapolis: NIP; London: Bodley Head, 1987, 498 pp.
Authoritative and analytical narrative, especially since 30-year rule prevented public record availability; on Falklands/Malvinas, pp. 356–85; reviewed potential "signal" of withdrawal of ENDURANCE; first sea lord Sir Henry Leach given credit for early optimism about prospects and possibilities for assembling the task force to recover the islands; noted that British used SAS men ashore and submarines at sea to report air sorties from Argentine mainland.

211   Gueritz, E. F. "The Falklands: Joint Warfare Justified." JRUSI, 127 (September 1982): 46–55.
Recapitulation of events of the campaign at the time.

212   Guest, Iain. BEHIND THE DISAPPEARANCES: ARGENTINA'S DIRTY WAR AGAINST HUMAN RIGHTS AND THE UNITED NATIONS. Philadelphia: Pennsylvania UP, 1990, 621 pp.
A political assessment of events of oppression during the 1970s; several references to the campaign.

213   Guinazu, Enrique Ruiz. PROAS DE ESPANA EN EL MAR MAGALLANICO. Buenos Aires, 1945.
Beautifully illustrated; reviewed Argentine claims.

214   Gunston, Bill. AN ILLUSTRATED GUIDE TO MILITARY HELICOPTERS. New York: Arco, 1981, 159 pp.
General reference information.

215   Gustafson, Lowell S. THE SOVEREIGNTY DISPUTE OVER THE FALKLAND (MALVINAS) ISLANDS. New York and Oxford: Oxford UP, 1988, 276 pp.
From Ph.D. dissertation [216]; noted dispute was over sovereignty; admitted Argentines had superior historical right; reviewed details on 1976 Shackleton mission and report [452];

BELGRANO controversy extended several years in British politics, one step being Clive Ponting trial; he was acquitted; Commons Foreign Affairs Committee [252] concluded that there was no link to Peruvian peace plan.

216 Gustafson, Lowell S. "The Sovereignty Dispute over the Falkland (Malvinas) Islands." Ph.D. diss., Virginia, 1984, 415 pp.
Ph.D. dissertation with research completed well after the campaign; studied various aspects of the dispute: claims, sovereignty, rights, self-determination, colonialism, and prospects for future.

217 Haffa, Annegret I. BEAGLE—KONFLIKT UND FALKLAND (MALVINEN)—KRIEG: ZUR AUSSENPOLITIK DER ARGENTINISCHEN MILITARREGIERUNG 1976 BIS 1983 [BEAGLE CONFLICT AND THE FALKLAND/MALVINAS WAR: THE FOREIGN POLICY OF THE ARGENTINE MILITARY REGIME]. Cologne and Munich: Weltforum, 1987, 453 pp.
German study; linked contemporary diplomatic disputes involving Argentina.

218 Haig, Alexander M. CAVEAT: REALISM, REAGAN, AND FOREIGN POLICY. London: Weidenfeld & Nicolson, 1984, 380 pp.
Memoirs of the American secretary of state who conducted the shuttle diplomacy mission prior to the beginning of active fighting; quite candid about various positions of Argentine and British leaders and about rivalries within the Reagan administration, especially disagreements between Haig and Jeane Kirkpatrick; Haig blamed the White House staff for permitting the disagreements to persist, all to sustain the popularity of Reagan, he claimed; "The Falklands War cost me my job as Secretary of State" (p. 298).

219 Halperin, Morton H. LIMITED WAR: AN ESSAY ON THE DEVELOPMENT OF THE THEORY AND AN ANNOTATED BIBLIOGRAPHY. OCCASIONAL PAPERS # 3. New York: AMS, 1962, 1973, 73 pp.
A paper for the Center for International Affairs, Harvard University.

220 Halperin, Morton H. LIMITED WAR IN THE NUCLEAR AGE. New York: Wiley, 1963, 200 pp.

Self-imposed limitations for warfare by the superpowers, Korea being the case study; 343 entries in the annotated bibliography.

221   Hamilton, John. THE HELICOPTER STORY OF THE FALK-LANDS CAMPAIGN. London: David & Charles, n.d.
Told the story of helicopter operations in paintings; four years of research on sites in the Falklands/Malvinas.

222   Hanrahan, Brian, and Fox, Robert. "I COUNTED THEM ALL OUT AND I COUNTED THEM ALL BACK": THE BATTLE FOR THE FALKLANDS. PORTWAY BOOK. Bath: Chivers, 1982, 187 pp.
One of the most famous accounts by participating journalists; title became memorable as assurance of survivability of Harriers during early sorties and a hint of censorship problems.

223   Harmon, Kenneth. "Blind Man's Bluff: Professional Notes." NIProc, 116 (July 1990): 69–72.
Called for the need for more effective identification, friend or foe, e.g., loss of SHEFFIELD partly due to confusion over identification.

224   HARPER'S MAGAZINE. A monthly newsmagazine. New York.
Consistent coverage of the campaign.

225   Harris, Robert. GOTCHA!: THE MEDIA, THE GOVERN-MENT, AND THE FALKLANDS CRISIS. Boston and London: Faber & Faber, 1983, 158 pp.
The most notable of the analyses of media-government relations during the campaign; the title was from THE SUN headline reporting the sinking of BELGRANO on 3 May, the most famous headline of the campaign—although the headline was removed immediately after the first edition and another was substituted, "Did 1200 Argies Drown?"; claimed, to some extent, there was a "war" between Fleet Street, the government, the Ministry of Defence, and the broadcasters; concluded that the censorship process was incompetent.

226   Hart-Davis, Duff. ASCENSION: THE STORY OF A SOUTH ATLANTIC ISLAND. London: Constable, 1972, 256 pp.

Some details on this "useless" island, originally a cable and wireless station up to the time of publication.

227   Hartman, Tom and Mitchell, John. A WORLD ATLAS OF MILITARY HISTORY, 1945–1984. London: Leo Cooper, 1984, 117 pp.
On the post–World War II period; section on "The Recapture of the Falkland Islands, 1982," pp. 86–87.

228   Hastings, Max and Jenkins, Simon. LA BATALLA POR LAS MALVINAS. Buenos Aires: Emece Editores, 1983, 393 pp.
Spanish translation of [229].

229   Hastings, Max and Jenkins, Simon. THE BATTLE FOR THE FALKLANDS. New York and London: Norton, 1983, 393 pp.
Probably the most popular and distinguished of the accounts by participating journalists, Hastings, with Jenkins reporting on the home front; numerous printings and Spanish translation [228]; reviewed background, noting Julian Amery was "hardest of the hard-liners" supporting the Falklands Lobby; detailed the process of obtaining passage of the U.N. Resolution 502 calling for Argentine withdrawal; described the "media war," the most controversially reported conflict since 1945.

230   Headland, Robert K. CHRONOLOGICAL LIST OF ANT-ARCTIC EXPEDITIONS AND RELATED HISTORICAL EVENTS. STUDIES IN POLAR RESEARCH. Cambridge: Cambridge UP, 1989, 740 pp.
By the archivist, Scott Polar Research Institute, Cambridge; the definitive record of over 3,300 expeditions including several associated with exploration and discovery of the Falklands/Malvinas.

231   Headland, Robert K. THE ISLAND OF SOUTH GEORGIA. New York and Cambridge: Cambridge UP, 1984, 309 pp.
About the discovery, in 1675, and geography of this "dependency."

232   Henderson, Sir Nicholas. "America and the Falklands: Case Study in the Behavior of an Ally." THE ECONOMIST (12 November 1983): 31-38.

By the British ambassador to the U.S.; recalled the extraordinary interest among Americans; some details of circumstances of the BELGRANO sinking, claiming that Argentina was warned sufficiently prior to the act.

233   Henry, Harry. BEHIND THE HEADLINES: THE BUSINESS OF THE BRITISH PRESS. London: Associated Business, 1978.
A general review of processes of newspaper reporting.

234   Hickling, Harold. SAILOR AT SEA. London: Kimber, 1965, 224 pp.
Memoirs of a young officer at the battle of the Falklands.

235   Hilditch, A. Neville. CORONEL AND THE FALKLAND ISLANDS. London: Oxford UP, 1915, 37 pp.
One of the earliest accounts of the battle of the Falklands.

236   Hill, J. R. AIR DEFENCE AT SEA. London: Allan, 1988, 112 pp.
By admiral, RN; included an assessment of the Falklands/Malvinas campaign.

237   Hill, J. R. BRITISH SEA POWER IN THE 1980s. London: Allan, 1985, 128 pp.
Large picture book reviewing various dimensions of sea warfare, the Royal Marines, women in the navy, and some observations about the Falklands/Malvinas campaign.

238   Hill, J. R. MARITIME STRATEGY FOR MEDIUM POWERS. London: Croom Helm, 1986, 247 pp.
By admiral, RN; presented strategic background and planning for a general strategy for the future for Great Britain, the transition from an independent to a dependent stance.

239   Hill, J. R. THE ROYAL NAVY: TODAY AND TOMORROW. London: Allan, 1981, 1982, 144 pp.
Large picture book for a general audience to "show-case" the RN; completed before the campaign.

240   Hodges, Donald C. ARGENTINA, 1943–1987: THE NATIONAL REVOLUTION AND RESISTANCE. Albuquerque: U New Mexico P, 1976, 1988, 360 pp.
An up-to-date textbook on recent Argentine history.

241 Hoffmann, Fritz Leo and Hoffmann, Olga Mingo. SOVER-
EIGNTY IN DISPUTE: THE FALKLANDS/MALVINAS, 1493–
1982. SPECIAL STUDIES. Boulder, CO: Westview, 1984, 208
pp.
  A review of the salient events associated with exploration,
settlement, and claims of the islands.

242 Holmes, Deborah. GOVERNING THE PRESS: MEDIA FREE-
DOM IN THE UNITED STATES AND GREAT BRITAIN. SPE-
CIAL STUDIES. Boulder, CO: Westview, 1986, 116 pp.
  Comparative approach; noted newspapers were more compe-
titive in Great Britain than in the U.S. and that the campaign
raised the level of that competition; included many interviews
with participants; details on role of BBC which was criticized
by the government and MPs for being "insufficiently patriotic";
concluded that the newspapers refused to criticize the government but, nevertheless, the government treated the media as an
inconvenience.

243 Honeywell, Martin and Pearce, Jenny, eds. FALKLANDS/
MALVINAS: WHOSE CRISIS? London: Latin American Bureau,
1982, 141 pp.
  Compilation of essays; first SHACKLETON REPORT [452]
described degenerating, demoralized, and impoverished society;
presented Argentine perspectives; noted that both sides were
responsible.

244 Hooper, Alan. THE MILITARY AND THE MEDIA. Aldershot, England: Gower, 1982, 262 pp.
  By a serving officer, Royal Marines; on media-armed forces relations; could learn lessons from U.S.-Vietnam experience, Northern Ireland-army, the Iranian embassy affair, and the Falklands/
Malvinas campaign, one of the best examples from which to
learn; concluded that the Ministry of Defence handled media
relations poorly.

245 Hopple, Gerald W. "Intelligence and Warning: Implications
and Lessons of the Falkland Islands War." WORLD POLITICS, 37
(April 1984): 339–61.
  Comparative case studies: German attack on Russia in 1941,
Pearl Harbor, and North Korean attack on South Korea.

246 Hough, Richard A. THE PURSUIT OF ADMIRAL VON
SPEE: A GALLANT ENEMY MEETS THE ROYAL NAVY AT
THE END OF A CLASSIC SEA CHASE. New York: Harper &
Row; London: Allen & Unwin, 1969, 180 pp.
On the battle of the Falklands with much from the German
perspective.

247 House of Commons. THE FALKLANDS CAMPAIGN: A
DIGEST OF DEBATES IN THE HOUSE OF COMMONS, 2 APRIL
TO 15 JUNE 1982. London: HMSO, 1982, 361 pp.
Digest of six full debates and many questions and statements;
House of Lords debates not included; informative annexes added,
e.g., on performance of weapons systems and statistics on losses.

248 House of Commons. Defence Committee. THE FUTURE
DEFENCE OF THE FALKLAND ISLANDS. Third Report, Session
1982–1983. London: HMSO, May 1983.
Preparation for "Fortress Falklands."

249 House of Commons. Defence Committee. THE HANDLING
OF PRESS AND PUBLIC INFORMATION DURING THE FALK-
LANDS CONFLICT. First Report, Session 1982–1983. 2 vols.
London: HMSO, December 1982.
The result of all of the controversy over media–Ministry of
Defence relations; an extensive study and detailed report; topics
and themes included: Official Secrets Act, D-Notices, "off-the-
record" briefings, censorship, and provisions for journalists at
the front.

250 House of Commons. Defence Committee. THE HANDLING
OF PRESS AND PUBLIC INFORMATION DURING THE FALK-
LANDS CONFLICT. OBSERVATIONS PRESENTED BY THE
SECRETARY OF STATE FOR DEFENCE. Session 1982–1983,
Cmnd 8820. London: HMSO, March 1983.
The response from the Ministry of Defence to the Defence
Committee report [249].

251 House of Commons. Foreign Affairs Committee. FALK-
LAND ISLANDS. Fifth Report, Session 1983–1984. 2 vols. London:
HMSO, October 1984, 251 pp.
The report, minutes of meetings, and lists of witnesses.

252 House of Commons. Foreign Affairs Committee. EVENTS OF THE WEEKEND OF 1ST AND 2ND MAY 1982. Report of the Committee, Session 1984–1985. London: HMSO, 1985.

The occasion of the BELGRANO sinking which precipitated an enormous controversy; see account of Gavshon [192] for sensationalist perspective; the investigation and report of the committee.

253 House of Commons. Foreign Affairs Committee. FALK-LAND ISLANDS INQUIRY. Second Special Report, Session, 1982–1983. London: HMSO, May 1983, 4 pp.

The general investigation and report.

254 Howat, J.N.T. FALKLAND ISLANDS MAILS: THE KOS-MOS YEARS WITH THE DEUTSCHE DAMPFSCHIFFAHRTS GESELLSCHAFT "KOSMOS" OF HAMBURG. London: British Philatelic Trust, 1989, 160 pp.

A particular feature of Falklands/Malvinas philatelic efforts.

255 Hoyt, Edwin P. CARRIER WARS: NAVAL AVIATION FROM WORLD WAR 2 TO THE PERSIAN GULF. New York: McGraw-Hill, 1989, 284 pp.

Included section on Falklands/Malvinas campaign (pp. 251–52) but with howlers: aircraft from Argentine carrier sank ARDENT and then called that "the greatest shock of the sea war in the Falklands."

256 Hoyt, Edwin P. DEFEAT AT THE FALKLANDS: GER-MANY'S EAST ASIA SQUADRON, 1914. London: Hale, 1981, 240 pp.

By popular history writer who presented the German perspective on the campaign culminating in the battle of the Falklands of 1914.

257 Huertas, Alsvador Mafe and Briasco, Jesus Romero. ARGENTINE AIR FORCES IN THE FALKLANDS CONFLICT. WARBIRDS ILLUSTRATED # 45. New York: Sterling; London: Arms & Armour, 1987, 72 pp.

Details on types of aircraft including helicopters; incomplete information; focused on Super Etendards and EXOCET missiles; claimed that during the period 2 April to 14 June the Argentine air force clocked 12,454 flight-hours, about 3000 in combat, 452 landings at Stanley airport, and 796 helicopter missions.

258 Humble, Richard. AIRCRAFT CARRIERS: THE ILLUSTRATED HISTORY. London: Joseph, 1982, 192 pp.
Numerous illustrations; authoritative and well-researched.

259 Humble, Richard. THE RISE AND FALL OF THE BRITISH NAVY. London: Queen Anne, 1986, 255 pp.
Called the RN an "instrument of survival from 1509 to 1919, then demolition from 1945 to 1985"; throughout there is continuous shrill indictment for the mistakes of the "fall" period; strident, didactic, judgmental, using every opportunity for Cold War rhetoric; much Mountbatten-bashing; the Falklands/Malvinas campaign "came almost in the disguise of a blessing" (p. 8) and was "an irrelevant war" (p. 11); called STUFT "massive press-gang raids" to obtain a fleet train (p. 225); subsequently the RN has been betrayed, e.g., no replacements for lost units.

260 Informe Oficial Ejercito Argentino. CONFLICTO MALVINAS. 1983.
Official report of the Argentine army in the conflict.

261 INTELLIGENCE AND NATIONAL SECURITY. A quarterly periodical. London: Frank Cass.
Several important articles on intelligence aspects of the campaign in this professional journal.

262 INTERNATIONAL AFFAIRS. A quarterly review for the Royal Institute of International Affairs. Guilford: Butterworth Scientific.
Several articles on the diplomacy of the preliminaries to the campaign.

263 International Institute for Strategic Studies. "The Falklands War: Military Lessons of the Falklands Campaign." Strategic Survey, 1982–1983. Cambridge: IISS, 1983, 116–23.
A think-tank study and assessment.

264 Irving, Edmund. "Does Withdrawal of ENDURANCE Signal a Falklands Desertion?" GEOGRAPHICAL MAGAZINE, 54 (January 1982): 3–4.

By the former hydrographer of the navy who speculated months before the fact about "signals" and the withdrawal of ENDURANCE; an early reference to the upcoming 150th anniversary of British colonization; noted widespread concern.

265 Irving, John James. CORONEL AND THE FALKLANDS. London: Philpot, 1927, 247 pp.
A considered, authoritative study of the battles in 1914.

266 Jackson, John. "From Inchon to San Carlos: Amphibious Warfare since 1945." DEFENCE FORCE JOURNAL, 76 (May 1989): 47–57.
A survey of recent activities in amphibious warfare.

267 JANE'S ALL THE WORLD'S AIRCRAFT. Yearbook, various dates, e.g., 1979–1980. London: Jane's, 1979, 820 pp.
Since 1909; included sections on Argentina and the U.K.; extremely useful and informative reference work for all levels, including intelligence.

268 JANE'S FIGHTING SHIPS. Yearbook, various dates, e.g., 1981-1982; 1982–1983; 1983–1984. London: Jane's, various, e.g., 794 pp.; 779 pp.; 855 pp.
Since 1897; the most prestigious and authoritative naval yearbook presenting detailed summaries with photographs of all of the warships of all of the navies of the world; e.g., the 1990–1991 edition was edited by Richard Sharp, cost 110 pounds (c. $200), and, like its predecessors, included a critical editorial, in this case denouncing the procurement policies of the RN; a typical scenario for virtually everyone interested or involved in the Falklands/Malvinas campaign, apparently even including intelligence officials, would be to go to the appropriate issue of JANE'S, in this case, 1981–1982, and learn details about the naval capabilities of the RN and/or of the Argentine navy, more likely the latter.

269 JANE'S NAVAL REVIEW. London: Jane's, various, 160 pp.
Since 1981, original title, JANE'S NAVAL ANNUAL; not the same as RUSI AND BRASSEY'S DEFENCE YEARBOOK [440]; in

1981-1983 edition, essay by John Moore, "The Lessons of the Naval War in the Falklands," pp. 14–23; noted lack of airborne early warning, frequent severe fires, and the spectacular performance of the Harriers.

270 Jenkins, Peter. MRS. THATCHER'S REVOLUTION: THE ENDING OF THE SOCIALIST ERA. London: Cape; Cambridge, MA: Harvard UP, 1987, 1988, 1989, 453 pp.

A political biography; section on Falklands/Malvinas and "Falklands factor" (pp. 159–65), which Jenkins played down; claimed the government was gaining popularity beginning in December 1981.

271 Jenkins, Simon. "Britain's Pearl Harbor: The Falklands War." SUNDAY TIMES (22 March and 29 March 1987): 29 and 45–46.

Allusion to surprise attack; claimed the Argentine invasion was the result of extensive planning and, thus, demonstrated a major failure in British and American intelligence; accused Downing Street of not listening to warnings which were raised; general cynical tone.

272 Jofre, Oscar Luis and Aguiar, Felix R. MALVINAS: LA DEFENSA DE PUERTO ARGENTINO. Buenos Aires: Sudamericana, 1987, 325 pp.

An account of the campaign.

273 Johnson, Franklyn A. DEFENCE BY MINISTRY: THE BRITISH MINISTRY OF DEFENCE, 1944–1974. New York: Holmes & Meier, 1980, 253 pp.

Foreword by Earl Mountbatten; by an American academic; study of the structural reorganization of the defense forces after World War II; subsequent companion to earlier study of the Committee of Imperial Defence.

274 Johnson, Richard, "The Future of the Falkland Islands." WORLD TODAY, 33 (June 1977): 223–31.

By member of Shackleton I study group [452] to determine economic potential; Argentines refused to accept the report.

275 Johnson, Samuel. THOUGHTS IN THE LATE TRANSACTIONS RESPECTING FALKLAND ISLANDS. London: n.p., 1771.

A political pamphlet to persuade MPs in the late eighteenth century when decisions were being made about settling the Falkland Islands.

276 Jolly, Rick. THE RED AND GREEN LIFE MACHINE: A DIARY OF THE FALKLANDS FIELD HOSPITAL. London: Century; London: Corgi, 1983, 1984, 156 pp.

Claimed to be the first book about the campaign by a non-journalist; diary from 5 March to 11 July focusing on a field hospital unit.

277 Jordan, Gerald, ed. BRITISH MILITARY HISTORY: A SUPPLEMENT TO ROBIN HIGHAM'S GUIDE TO THE SOURCES. MILITARY HISTORY BIBLIOGRAPHIES series, # 10. New York: Garland, 1988, 600 pp.

6400 entries, supplementing an older standard bibliography; coverage on campaign in Barry Hunt essay, pp. 317–43.

278 Jordan, John. "Loosening the Stranglehold on the Royal Navy." NIProc, 115 (March 1989): 34–39.

Noted crisis in RN after 1981 White Paper and, even after Falklands/Malvinas campaign, promises of 50 destroyer-types not fulfilled; no orders for new ships.

279 Junor, Penny. MARGARET THATCHER: WIFE, MOTHER, POLITICIAN. London: Sidgwick & Jackson, 1983, 224 pp.

A personal biography; on Falklands/Malvinas campaign, pp. 158–68.

280 Jusid, Juan Jose. ASESINATO EN EL SENADO DE LA NACION. Movie. n.d.

An allegorical critique of Argentine government and society to raise political consciousness.

281 Jusid, Juan Jose. LA ROSALES. Movie. n.d.

An allegorical critique of Argentine government and society; in this case an attack on the officer corps; how naval officers were cowardly and abandoned their men.

282 Kanaf, Leo. LA BATALLA DE LAS MALVINAS. Buenos Aires: Tribuna Abierta, 1982, 212 pp.

Rush to publication; published in June 1982; obviously compiled in haste; recalled previous British naval battles in the vicinity; exaggerated the British losses in the Falklands/Malvinas campaign; cover picture of British destroyer exploding.

283   Kaufman, Chaim. U.S. MEDIATION IN THE FALKLANDS /MALVINAS CRISIS: SHUTTLE DIPLOMACY IN THE 1980s. Pittsburgh: Pew Program, 1988.
Account of U.S. efforts at settlement including the Haig shuttle diplomacy.

284   Kavanagh, Dennis A. and Seldon, Anthony, eds. THE THACHER EFFECT: A DECADE OF CHANGE. New York: Oxford UP, 1989, 376 pp.
A collection of essays; little on campaign.

285   Kavanagh, Dennis A. THATCHERISM AND BRITISH POLITICS: THE END OF CONSENSUS? New York and Oxford: Oxford UP, 1987, 1990, 352 pp.
Little on the campaign but some on how Thatcher gained power and control because of it.

286   Kempton, Murray. "General Galtieri's Case." NEW YORK REVIEW OF BOOKS, 29 (15 July 1982): 23–24.
Not what it claimed; a cynical description of Galtieri, who "modelled himself on Mussolini in World War II" and bragged about fighting to the last man.

287   Kennedy, Paul M. THE RISE AND FALL OF BRITISH NAVAL MASTERY. New York: Scribners; London: Allen Lane, 1976, 1982, 1986, 405 pp.
The best historical survey of maritime power, or naval mastery, as he called it, in Great Britain; "sets the RN within a framework of national, international, economic, political, and strategical considerations"; began with sixteenth century; British sea power was a factor of economic and strategic power; when one fluctuated, so did the other.

288   Kiely, David G. NAVAL ELECTRONIC WARFARE. SEA POWER series # 5. Washington and London: Brasseys, 1987, 1988, 136 pp.

Foreword by Sir Edward Ashmore; a general historical survey.

289 Kiely, David G. NAVAL SURFACE WEAPONS. SEA POW-
ER series # 6. Washington and London: Brassey's, 1988, 113 pp.
Details on various weapons systems; part of a series.

290 King, David E. "Intelligence Failures and the Falklands
War: A Reassessment." INTELLIGENCE AND NATIONAL SE-
CURITY, 2 (April 1987): 336–40.
Reaction to the article by L. Freedman [174]; apologist for
British authorities; noted that FRANKS REPORT [168], which
attached no blame to the government, did criticize intelligence
aspects; it is now clear, said King, that perfect intelligence would
not have changed events; cited RATTENBACH REPORT [422]
which noted that planning for the Argentine invasion occurred
within a small group and, even then, the execution date was
moved up by several months.

291 Kinney, Douglas. NATIONAL INTEREST/NATIONAL
HONOR: THE DIPLOMACY OF THE FALKLANDS CRISIS. Institute for the Study of Diplomacy, Georgetown University.
Westport, CT: Praeger, 1989, 392 pp.
By specialist in foreign affairs; chronological study of origins
and nature of the crisis; long list of possible methods of resolution
and there was sufficient time (1000 hours) for proper negotiation,
yet war ensued.

292 Kirkpatrick, Jeane J. DICTATORSHIPS AND DOUBLE
STANDARDS: RATIONALISM AND REASON IN POLITICS.
American Enterprise Institute. New York: Simon & Schuster,
1982, 270 pp.
A series of essays and lectures sponsored by the prominent
conservative think-tank.

293 Kirkpatrick, Jeane J. LEADER AND VANGUARD IN MASS
SOCIETY: A STUDY OF PERONIST ARGENTINA. Cambridge:
MIT UP, 1971, 286 pp.
An academic study of Argentina in the decades after World
War II.

294 Kirkpatrick, Jeane J. "My Falklands War and Theirs." NA-
TIONAL INTEREST, 18 (Winter 1989–1990): 11-20.

Kirkpatrick's review of Charlton book [91] and her observations on the Falklands/Malvinas campaign; she concluded the war was a heroic response to a wholly unwarranted act of aggression; admitted that her views and actions were at odds to those of secretary of state Haig; assessed journalist-created dichotomy of "hard liners" and "pragmatists" (Kirkpatrick and Haig, respectively) as "silly"; her concern was good hemispheric relations; concluded that the U.S. emerged from the affair weakened in Latin America and no stronger in Europe.

295   Kitson, Linda. Exhibition at the Imperial War Museum. November 1982.

94 drawings from her experiences during the Falklands/Malvinas campaign; sponsored by the Artistic Records Committee; exhibition then went on tour.

296   Kitson, Linda. THE FALKLANDS WAR: A VISUAL DIARY. London: Mitchell Beasley, 1982.

Commissioned drawings by the official war artist.

297   Koburger, Charles W., Jr. SEA POWER IN THE FALKLANDS. SPECIAL STUDY. New York: Praeger, 1983, 202 pp.

By a captain of the U.S. Coast Guard; details on naval forces and operations.

298   Kon, Daniel. LOS CHICOS DE LA GUERRA: HABLAN LOS SOLDADOS QUE ESTUVIERON EN MALVINAS. Buenos Aires: Editorial Galerina, 1982, 1983, 222 pp.

A much-acclaimed and popular oral history of the life of eight Argentine soldier-conscripts during the campaign; translated into English [300]; made into a movie [299]; accounts of horrible conditions, muddle, neglect, hunger, and terror; officers did little for them; an indictment of incompetence and heartlessness against the Junta.

299   Kon, Daniel and Kamin, Bebe. LOS CHICOS DE LA GUER-RA. A Movie. London Film Festival, 1984.

A feature film made from the oral history by Kon [298], a journalist who interviewed several returned conscripts.

300   Kon, Daniel. CONSCRIPTS OF THE WAR. London: New English, 1983, 222 pp.

English translation of [298].

301 Labougle, Raul de. LA CUESTION MALVINAS EN LAS NACIONES UNIDAS. Buenos Aires: Casa Pardo, 1965, 63 pp.
A review of the U.S. involvement in the issues two decades before the campaign.

302 Ladd, James D. INSIDE THE COMMANDOS: A PICTO-RIAL HISTORY FROM WORLD WAR TWO TO THE PRESENT. Annapolis: NIP, 1984, 160 pp.
Over 400 illustrations; a history of operations over the past 50 years, e.g., Dieppe, Aden, Suez, and the Falklands/Malvinas campaign.

303 Ladd, James D. THE ROYAL MARINES, 1919–1980. AN AUTHORIZED HISTORY. New York and London: Jane's, 1980, 482 pp.
Foreword by HRH Prince Philip; a substantial history including amphibious and commando operations.

304 Ladd, James D. SBS: THE INVISIBLE RAIDERS: THE HIS-TORY OF THE SPECIAL BOAT SQUADRON FROM WORLD WAR II TO THE PRESENT. Annapolis: NIP; London: Arms & Armour, 1983, 1984, 283 pp.
Foreword by P. G. Davis; detailed history of numerous operations from the Mediterranean early in World War II and in the Far East later, and finally, in the Falklands/Malvinas campaign, pp. 219–44; recovery of South Georgia an exclusive achievement.

305 Laffin, John. BRASSEY'S BATTLES: 3500 YEARS OF CON-FLICTS, CAMPAIGNS AND WARS FROM A - Z. Washington and London: Brassey's, 1986, 497 pp.
Over 7000 battles recounted; the Falklands/Malvinas, pp. 163–65; described as an imperial nineteenth-century type of conflict.

306 Laffin, John. FIGHT FOR THE FALKLANDS!: WHY AND HOW BRITAIN AND ARGENTINA WENT TO WAR—FROM INVASION TO SURRENDER. New York: St. Martins; Bath: Chivers, 1982, 225 pp.
By a prolific military historian; published in September; also paperback version; from British perspective; no scholarly apparatus, table of contents, or index.

307   Laffin, John. "The Truth about the BELGRANO." SPECTA-TOR (11 June 1983).
A short assessment one year after the event.

308   LaFrance, David G. and Jones, Errol D. LATIN AMERI-CAN MILITARY HISTORY: AN ANNOTATED BIBLIOGRA-PHY. MILITARY HISTORY BIBLIOGRAPHIES series # 12. New York: Garland, 1991, 500 pp.
12 chapters covering from 1492 to the present.

309   LA PRENSA. Daily newspaper. Buenos Aires.
Popular and influential Argentine newspaper; in the months before the invasion, e.g., on 24 January and 7 February 1982, contained warnings that if the New York talks broke down, Argentina would resort to force.

310   Larson, Everette E. A SELECTIVE LISTING OF MONO-GRAPHS AND GOVERNMENT DOCUMENTS ON THE FALK-LAND/MALVINAS ISLANDS OF THE LIBRARY OF CON-GRESS. HISPANIC FOCUS series # 1. Washington: Library of Congress, 1982, 28 pp.
A product of research among the holdings of the Library of Congress; 196 entries including 149 monographs plus government documents.

311   Latin American Newsletters. THE FALKLANDS WAR: THE OFFICIAL HISTORY, OFFICIAL COMMUNIQUES. Latin American Newsletters, 1983.
A semi-official compilation.

312   Laver, Margaret Patricia Henwood. AN ANNOTATED BIB-LIOGRAPHY OF THE FALKLAND ISLANDS AND THE FALK-LAND ISLANDS DEPENDENCIES. UNIVERSITY OF CAPE TOWN LIBRARIES BIBLIOGRAPHICAL SERIES. Cape Town: U Cape Town Libraries, 1974, 1977, 266 pp.
1539 entries; an updated collection sponsored by the University of Cape Town.

313   Lawrence, John and Lawrence, Robert. WHEN THE FIGHT-ING IS OVER: A PERSONAL STORY OF THE BATTLE OF TUMBLEDOWN MOUNTAIN AND ITS AFTERMATH. London: Bloomsbury, 1988, 208 pp.

The narrative for a BBC-TV fictionalized play.

314 Layman, C.H. "Duty in Bomb Alley." NIProc, 109 (August 1983): 35–40.

By a captain, RN; commanding officer of ARGONAUT, a LEANDER-Class frigate, which suffered several bomb attacks and sustained much damage.

315 Lebow, Richard Led. "Miscalculations in the South Atlantic: The Origins of the Falkland War." JOURNAL OF STRATEGIC STUDIES, 6 (March 1983): 5–35.

The two mistakes were the British belief that Argentina would not invade and the Argentine belief that the British would acquiesce to the invasion; all was illusion; an air of unreality which led to "an OPERA BOUFFE conflict"; the U.S. policy also misled Argentina.

316 Lehman, John F., Jr. COMMAND OF THE SEAS. New York: Scribners, 1988, 476 pp.

By former secretary of the navy of the U.S.; chapter on the campaign, pp. 269–90; noted longtime cooperation and coordination of Anglo-American naval activities and agencies; proved to be decisive in the campaign, he claimed; reviewed various types of operations.

317 Lewis, Brenda Ralph. "Fortress Falklands." NIProc, 110 (March 1984): 151–54.

Second year review; the Falklands/Malvinas was transformed from an unconsidered colony to a heavily defended fortress; still, there was no armistice and no treaty.

318 Lewis, Brenda Ralph. "The Loss of HMS COVENTRY." NIProc, 110 (September 1984): 141-43.

The Type-42 destroyer lost on 25 May while engaged in the advanced air defense screen protecting the carriers.

319 Lider, Julian. BRITISH MILITARY THOUGHT AFTER WORLD WAR II. Brookfield, VT, and Aldershot: Gower, 1985, 633 pp.

Assessment of the nature of war, strategic studies, and current policy since World War II; named a number of formulators of strategic thought; noted the influence of military periodicals and think-tanks; sections on Suez and the Falklands/Malvinas campaign, pp. 248–54.

320 Little, Walter. "The Falklands Affair: A Review of the Literature." POLITICAL STUDIES, 32 (1984): 296–310.

By U. Liverpool academic; reviewed diplomatic background and roles of Britain, Argentina, and the U.S.; commended FRANKS REPORT [168] as informative on the background even if the final conclusion was "absurd"; noted Haig-Kirkpatrick dispute, both apparently given free reign by a lax president and a lackluster National Security Agency.

321 LONDON GAZETTE. Supplements. London, various.

The traditional method for the commander to report operations and award honors for military and naval operations; John Fieldhouse's "Despatches" of 8 October and 13 December 1982 were full of interesting detail and 140 citations.

322 Luria, Rene. "The Argentine Military and Industry Confront the Crisis." INTERNATIONAL DEFENSE REVIEW, 23 (June 1990): 659–61.

A recent assessment; Argentina was especially hard hit economically due to debts, the Juntas, and the campaign; nevertheless, the navy remained intent on modernizing; the heroism of the navy pilots and the marines saved its honor; recounted completion of aviation plans.

323 MacFarlane, L. J. ISSUES IN BRITISH POLITICS SINCE 1945. New York and London: Longman, 1975, 1981, 1986, 160 pp.

Third edition of this general survey of economic, social, and external issues.

324 McGowan, Robert and Hands, Jeremy. DON'T CRY FOR ME, SERGEANT–MAJOR. London: Futura, 1983, 1985, 1986, 317 pp.

Admitted in the preface that this was a journalistic not a scholarly or individual account; "a unique portrait of the Falklands war—from the sharp end"; a record of the experiences of 10,000 men and women; concentrated on the army and marine activities; Lawrence Freedman [170] called it "a trivial pot-boiler."

325 McManners, Hugh, FALKLANDS COMMANDO. London: Kimber; London: Grafton, 1984, 1987, 320 pp.
By a captain of the Royal Artillery; a "worm's eye view" written two years later; illustrated memoirs.

326 Makin, Guillermo A. "Argentine Approaches to the Falklands/Malvinas: Was the Resort to Force Foreseeable?" INTERNATIONAL AFFAIRS, 59 (Summer 1983): 391–404.
By a Cambridge student; noted interpretations highlighting a series of warlike actions of the Argentines since the Peronist era; but, look more carefully, because only military regimes have been aggressive; the latest Junta contemplated military action to detract from internal difficulties; in conclusion, all of this meant a spectacular failure of British intelligence.

327 Makin, Guillermo A. "The Military in Argentine Politics, 1880–1982." MILLENNIUM, 12 (Spring 1983): 51–68.
An article reviewing military regimes during the last century in Argentina.

328 Marcella, Gabriel. THE MALVINAS/FALKLAND WAR OF 1982: LESSONS FOR THE UNITED STATES AND LATIN AMERICA. Carlisle Barracks, PA: Strategic Studies Institute, U.S. Army War College, 1983.
A strategic assessment by this U.S. army think-tank.

329 Marder, Arthur J. FROM DREADNOUGHT TO SCAPA FLOW: THE ROYAL NAVY IN THE FISHER ERA, 1904–1919. 5 vols. London: Oxford UP, 1961-1970, 1978, 1900 pp.
The standard account of the RN and the period prior to and during World War I; the battle of the Falklands in vol. II.

330 Marriott, Leo. ROYAL NAVY AIRCRAFT CARRIERS, 1945–1990. London: Allan, 1985, 144 pp.
Details on specifications, history, and operations; illustrated.

331 Marriott, Leo. ROYAL NAVY FRIGATES, 1845–1983. London: Allan, 1983, 128 pp.
Anti-submarine warfare ships larger than corvettes, e.g., TRIBAL and LEANDER classes, several of which operated in the campaign.

332   Marriott, Leo. TYPE 42. MODERN COMBAT SHIP series # 3. London: Allan, 1985, 112 pp.
There were 14 of these; some operated during the campaign, e.g., SHEFFIELD and COVENTRY, which were lost; interestingly, two Argentine destroyers were Type 42s; noted that lessons learned during the campaign were incorporated by the British during refits.

333   Mason, Francis K. HARRIER. Cambridge: Stephens, 1981, 1983, 200 pp.
Details on this VSTOL aircraft which was so successful during the campaign; second edition incorporated coverage of campaign, pp. 135–45.

334   Mason, R. A. " 'Hurray for the Hobby Horses': Reflections on the Air War in the South Atlantic, 1982." JRUSI, 127 (December 1982): 34–41.
By an air commodore, RAF; discussion of issues related to command of the air, including the Argentine air force, helicopters, and electronic warfare.

335   Meister, Jurg. DER KRIEG UM DIE FALKLAND-INSELN, 1982: GESCHICHTLICHE HINTERGRUNDE STRATEGIE UN TAKTIK DER KRIEGSFUHRUNG POLITISCH—WIRTSCHAFTLICHE PERSPEKTIVEN [THE WAR OF THE FALKLAND ISLANDS: HISTORICAL BACKGROUND OF THE STRATEGY AND TACTICS OF WARMAKING: POLITICAL AND ECONOMIC PERSPECTIVES]. Osnabruck: Biblio Verlag, 1984, 320 pp.
A German survey.

336   Melendez, Federico. THE FALKLANDS: A STUDY IN INTERNATIONAL CONFRONTATION. Carlsbad, CA: Arcadia, 1984, 466 pp.
Historical background from 1520 to 1820, then British rule, and then the campaign; was it to be Britain's last colonial war?

337   Menaul, Stewart W. B. "The Falklands Campaign: A War of Yesterday?" STRATEGIC REVIEW (Fall 1982): 82–91.
By an air vice-marshal; reviewed some operations; praise for the assembling of the task force; several errors, e.g., that BELGRANO

torpedoed by "unguided" torpedoes and that she was headed toward the task force.

338 Mercer, Derrik. "Is Press Freedom a Threat during National Crises?" JRUSI, 129 (September 1984): 38–42.
By former editor, THE SUNDAY TIMES; an edited paper given at a conference at Duke University, 1984; reviewed some problems of the media, claiming the Ministry of Defence was over-secretive and anti-media; the BBC had an advantage; noted commissioned study of the question by the Centre for Journalism Studies, Cardiff.

339 Metford, J.C.J. "Falklands or Malvinas? The Background to the Dispute." INTERNATIONAL AFFAIRS, 44 (July 1968): 463–81.
Chatham House review of the late 1960s; the essence of the dispute was over sovereignty, and for such an unprepossessing part of the world; the Argentine claim was founded on emotion and a recurrent irredentist fever; the British would like to dispossess themselves of their imperial past; there was no economic benefit involved.

340 Meyer, C. J. "LEANDER" CLASS. MODERN COMBAT SHIPS series # 1. London; Allan, 1984, 112 pp.
A modified Type 12 frigate, included 26 ships in three batches, plus others for the Dutch, Indian, Australian, and other navies.

341 Middlebrook, Martin. THE FIGHT FOR THE "MALVINAS": THE ARGENTINE FORCES IN THE FALKLANDS WAR. London: Viking, 1989, 321 pp.
This and the other Middlebrook account [342] were important additions to the literature; this one was the product of extensive research in Argentina several years after the campaign when he was finally granted a visa; enjoyed informative access to the Argentine navy and army but not the air force; 62 interviews not including Junta members, who were all in jail; a long narrative on the details of the BELGRANO sinking, pp. 98–116; claimed Argentine naval authorities were aware of changes to the Rules of Engagement and Exclusion Zones; described any criticism related to BELGRANO sinking as "humbug"; on the INVINCIBLE attack, the most controversial air action of the campaign, in fact, was

against AVENGER, and that EXOCET and bombs all missed, INVINCIBLE being 30 miles away; little on the role of the U.S.; informative footnotes but no sources cited and bibliography only a random listing of nine sources.

342 Middlebrook, Martin. OPERATION CORPORATE: THE FALKLANDS WAR, 1982. New York: Viking, 1985, 1986, 1987, 1989, 430 pp.

One of the most informative and interesting accounts, but strictly from the British perspective; used by the U.S. naval war college for wargaming the campaign; he has since completed an account from the Argentine perspective [341]; second edition included coverage of "blue-on-blue" incidents in which the British accidentally fired on own forces—he had been requested to remove those from the first edition.

343 Middlemas, Robert Keith. COMMAND OF THE FAR SEAS: A NAVAL CAMPAIGN OF THE FIRST WORLD WAR. London: Hutchinson, 1961, 255 pp.

Included battles of Coronel and the Falklands; he characterized the British-German roles during these early months as gamekeeper-poacher, respectively.

344 Milia, Fernando A. "The Argentine Navy Revisited." NAVAL HISTORY, 4 (Winter 1990): 24–29.

By rear admiral, Argentine navy; an account for naval "buffs."

345 MILLENNIUM: JOURNAL OF INTERNATIONAL STUDIES. A quarterly. London.

Special issue on the Falklands campaign, Spring 1983; seven articles, e.g., by Makin [327], Calvert [75], Doxey [133], and Windsor [528].

346 Millett, Allan R. and Williamson Murray, eds. MILITARY EFFECTIVENESS. 3 vols. Boston: Unwin Hyman, 1988, 996 pp.

Battle of the Falklands covered in vol. I on World War I; in his final assessment, Paul Kennedy noted that the battle of the Falklands was the last to be fought by gunfire alone, but he forgot the battle of the River Plate, fought nearby, in December 1939.

347 Milne, J. M. FLASHING BLADES OVER THE SEA. Liskeard: Maritime. n.d.

Introduction by the Prince of Wales; history of helicopters in the RN since 1943; 80 illustrations.

348 Ministry of Defence. THE BRITISH ARMY IN THE FALKLANDS, 1982. London: HMSO, 1982, 1983, 32 pp.
A commemorative booklet; color illustrated; some statistics.

349 Ministry of Defence. THE FALKLANDS CAMPAIGN: THE LESSONS. Secretary of State for Defence. Cmnd 8758. London: HMSO, 1982.
The Falklands White Paper published in December 1982; announced plans to replace lost equipment and reform policies based on lessons learned.

350 Ministry of Defence. OPERATION CORPORATE: ACHIEVEMENTS OF THE NAVAL SERVICE. Director of Naval Warfare. London: HMSO, 1982.
A commemorative pamphlet reviewing events.

351 Ministry of Defence. STATEMENT ON THE DEFENCE ESTIMATES, 1983. Cmnd 8951-1. London: HMSO, 1983.
To incorporate lessons from the campaign.

352 Ministry of Defence. THE UNITED KINGDOM DEFENCE PROGRAMME: THE WAY FORWARD. Cmnd 8288. London: HMSO, 1981.
The 1981 White Paper or Nott Defence Review making provision for such things as INVINCIBLE's sale to Australia, withdrawal of ENDURANCE, and destroyers/frigates to be reduced from 65 to 50.

353 Mitchell, Alastair. "The Development of Radar in the Royal Navy." 4 parts. WARSHIP, 2–14, 13–20, 117–34, 45–58, 218–31, 1980–1981.
Covers period 1935–1980.

354 Montenegro, Nestor J. and Aliverti, Eduardo. LOS NOMBRES DE LA DERROTA. Buenos Aires: Nemont Ediciones, 1982, 111 pp.
A series of interviews, including, it was claimed, "a fundamental protagonist," probably Galtieri, but no startling revelations.

355 Moore, Sir Jeremy and Woodward, Sir John. "The Falklands Experience." JRUSI, 128 (March 1983): 25–32.

By the commanders of the land and naval forces, respectively; from a lecture at RUSI; discussed Rules of Engagement, Exclusion Zones, and the press; noted that one problem with the press related to the first days of the campaign and the commanders were anxious to convince the Argentines that the British counter-invasion was beginning on 1 May, so some press information was either withheld or manipulated.

356 Moore, John E. "The Falklands Campaign: The Lessons." JANE'S NAVAL REVIEW, 1983–1984, 2 (1983): 9–20.

By the editor of JANE'S [268]; a review of the December 1982 White Paper on the lessons learned from the campaign; details on individual ships and classes, e.g., that aluminum superstructures of the Type 21 frigates were cracking excessively and that guns were to be added to the Type 22 class ships.

357 Moore, John E. and Compton-Hall, Richard. SUBMARINE WARFARE: TODAY AND TOMORROW. Bethesda, MD: Adler & Adler; London: Joseph, 1986, 1987, 320 pp.

A general historical review with projections into the future.

358 Moore, John E. WARSHIPS OF THE ROYAL NAVY. Annapolis: NIP; London: Macdonald & Jane's, 1979, 1981, 136 pp.

By the editor of JANE'S [268]; recalled an earlier compilation by Oscar Parkes; reviewed by classes such as carriers, destroyers, and submarines, and amphibious and mine warfare.

359 Moore, John Norton. "The Inter-American System Snarls in Falklands War." AMERICAN JOURNAL OF INTERNATIONAL LAW, 76 (October 1982): 830–31.

An assessment of the OAS, the oldest and most successful of regional organizations, but it failed in the Falklands/Malvinas campaign; the OAS voted to condemn Britain and urged support for Argentina.

360 Moorer, Thomas H. and Cottrell, Alvin J. "In the Wake of the Falklands Battle." STRATEGIC REVIEW (Summer 1982): 23–28.

By admiral, U.S. navy; serious deficiency in the campaign was lack of attack aircraft carriers, "the missing blanket of Air Protection"; there were other problems of logistics and damage control.

361 Moreno, Isidoro J. Ruiz. COMMANDOS EN ACCION: EL EJERCITO EN MALVINAS. Buenos Aires: Emece Editores, 1986, 460 pp.

Specialized Argentine forces, 601 and 602 Companies, who were to act as commandos and intelligence operatives, watching the Kelpers; account of the controversial incident involving the death of Colonel Herbert Jones, a British commander at Goose Green on 29 May; Lt. Gomez of 601 Commando claimed to have shot him while he was trying to trick soldiers into surrendering.

362 Moreno, Juan Carlos. LA RECUPERACION DE LAS MALVINAS. Buenos Aires: Plus Ultra, 1973, 313 pp.

An older account of hopes and aspirations.

363 Morgan, Kenneth O. THE PEOPLE'S PEACE: BRITISH HISTORY, 1945–1989. New York: Oxford UP, 1990, 572 pp.

A recent and thorough historical review of post–World War II Great Britain.

364 Morison, Samuel L. "The Falklands Campaign: A Chronology." NIProc, 109 (June 1983): 119–24.

Chronological listing with illustrations; useful and informative.

365 Morison, Samuel L. "The Falklands Campaign: A Chronology." WARSHIP INTERNATIONAL, 20 (1983): 376–98.

A useful chronological review.

366 Moro, Ruben O. LA GUERRA INAUDITA: HISTORIA DEL CONFLICTO DEL ATLANTICO SUR. Buenos Aires: Pleamar, 1985, 560 pp.

Original Spanish version of [367].

367 Moro, Ruben O. THE HISTORY OF THE SOUTH ATLANTIC CONFLICT: THE WAR OF THE MALVINAS. Westport, CT: Praeger, 1989, 1990, 380 pp.

By commodore of Argentine air force; headed Rattenbach Commission investigation [422]; the heroes of the conflict were the Argentine air force pilots, who gained worldwide admiration; believed the U.S. aid to the British was decisive; claimed several attacks on British warships not acknowledged, including INVINCIBLE.

368 Morrison, David E. and Tumber, Howard. JOURNALISTS AT WAR: THE DYNAMICS OF NEWS REPORTING DURING THE FALKLANDS CONFLICT. Newbury Park, CA and London: Sage, 1988, 384 pp.

Informative on how and why original journalists were selected—ultimately there were 30 representing 19 news organizations who accompanied the task force; about conflicts between and among journalists, e.g., most of the journalists resented Max Hastings but his reporting was quite successful; complaints about censorship; Ministry of Defence officials were called "minders."

369 Moxworthy, John L., ed. THE GREAT WHITE WHALE GOES TO WAR: CANBERRA. London: Peninsular & Orient, 1982, 192 pp.

By commander, RN; foreword by Captain D. J. Scott-Masson of SS CANBERRA; slick, heavy-paper format; unique story of a cruise liner which went to war, April-July 1982; 94 days at sea.

370 Mundo Lo, Sara de. THE FALKLAND/MALVINAS ISLANDS: A BIBLIOGRAPHY OF BOOKS, 1619–1982. Urbana, IL: Albatross, 1983, 68 pp.

On various aspects, exploration, wildlife, and the campaign (23 entries); 486 entries, some annotated, many in Spanish.

371 Murguizur, Juan Carlos. "The Future of the Submarine in Argentinian Naval Policy." INTERNATIONAL DEFENSE REVIEW, 17 (1984): 451-54.

By Argentine staff college lecturer; lessons from the campaign caused Argentine authorities to reevaluate the structure of the navy; previously it had been oriented toward anti-submarine warfare; in the campaign, arrival of British submarines forced withdrawal of the Argentine navy; similarly, British warships effectively ran from the small number of Argentine submarine attacks; thus, the decision to increase the number of submarines from four to six.

372 Murguizur, Juan Carlos. "The South Atlantic Conflict: An Argentinian Point of View." INTERNATIONAL DEFENSE REVIEW, 2 (February 1983): 135–40.

By Argentine military lecturer; presented "selective" chronology: included attempted Argentine submarine attack, 1 May;

British attempted landing and withdrawal (!), 2 May; nothing in chronology on BELGRANO (!); SHEFFIELD sunk and HERMES damaged (!) on 4 May; another Argentine submarine attack, 10 May; INVINCIBLE hit by EXOCET, 30 May (!); concluded that 38 British ships damaged including 2 carriers (!).

373 Myhre, Jeffrey D. "Title to the Falklands-Malvinas under International Law." MILLENNIUM, 12 (Spring 1983): 25–38.
Cited several cases of disputes over sovereignty; reviewed Spanish, French, and English discovery claims; British-Spanish dispute of 1771 led to the brink of war.

374 Myles, B. JUMP JET: THE REVOLUTIONARY V/S TOL FIGHTER. London: Brassey's, 1978, 1986, 298 pp.
Early survey of the Harrier.

375 NAVAL HISTORY. A quarterly journal. Annapolis: NIP.
A more popular journal of military history topics since 1988.

376 Naval Institute. NAVAL INSTITUTE GUIDE TO WORLD NAVAL WEAPONS SYSTEMS. Annapolis: NIP, 1989, 511 pp.
Compiled by Norman Friedman; biennial, alternate years with COMBAT FLEETS OF THE WORLD [101]; extensive coverage of guns, torpedoes, missiles, and command systems; assessed quality of systems.

377 NAVAL WAR COLLEGE REVIEW. A quarterly. Newport, RI.
Several articles on the campaign.

378 Newbolt, Henry. A NAVAL HISTORY OF THE WAR, 1914–1918. London: Hodder & Stoughton, n.d., 362 pp.
By the official historian; chapter 5 on the battle of the Falklands.

379 NEWSWEEK. Weekly newsmagazine. New York.
Ran four cover stories, 19 April to 31 May 1982; sample titles: "The Empire Strikes Back" and "The British Go In."

380 NEW YORK REVIEW OF BOOKS. A review, 22 times a year. New York.
Timely reviews and commentary.

381 Nicholas, Sir David. "The Services and the Media: Thoughts on the Future." AQDJ, 120 (July 1990): 261-68.

By chair, ITV News; reviewed recent sensational global events and recalled Falklands/Malvinas campaign; only three pieces of hostilities footage were broadcast during the campaign; all else was shown afterwards; SIR GALAHAD hit on 8 June, not broadcast until 24 June; complained about restrictions imposed by Ministry of Defence.

382 Nielsson, Gunnar. MEDIATION UNDER CRISIS MAN-AGEMENT CONDITIONS: THE UNITED NATIONS SECRE-TARY GENERAL AND THE FALKLAND/MALVINAS ISLANDS CRISIS APRIL 1–JUNE 14, 1982. Pittsburgh: Pew Program, 1983.
Diplomatic review; emphasis on one method.

383 Norman, Albert. THE FALKLAND ISLANDS, THEIR KIN-SHIP ISLES, THE ANTARCTIC HEMISPHERE, AND THE FREE-DOM OF TWO GREAT OCEANS: DISCOVERY AND DIPLOMA-CY, LAW AND WAR. Vol. I: THE ARGENTINIAN INVASION AND THE SEA AND LAND WARS, 1982. Northfield, VT: A. Norman, 1986, 632 pp.
On the campaign; highly personal and diverse observations; more volumes to follow.

384 Norris, Andrew and Beech, David. FALKLAND ISLANDS: THE "TRAVIS" FRANKS AND COVERS. London: Harmers, 1977, 29 pp.
By stamp auctioneers; about special editions; rare "black Frank" discovered.

385 Norton-Taylor, Richard. THE PONTING AFFAIR. London: Woolf, 1985, 144 pp.
About Clive Ponting, a Ministry of Defence official who leaked information; put on trial and acquitted; the trial demonstrated "valuable insights into culture and intrigue of Whitehall"; log of CONQUEROR lost; sensation about diary of seaman aboard CONQUEROR, used by Gavshon [192] but not identified.

386 Nott, John. "The Falklands Campaign." NIProc, 109 (May 1983): 118–39.
By former defence minister; edited version of White Paper of December 1982; Argentine invasion of 2 April was "an act of unprovoked aggression"; noted deficiencies in airborne early

warning; aluminum was not a factor in damage problems but cables and cable-ducts contributed significantly to the difficulties.

387 Nutwell, Robert M. "Postscript: The Falklands War." NIProc, 109 (January 1983): 82–83.

By commander, U.S. Navy; assessed issues of the anti-surface campaign waged by Argentine air force, sinking six ships; at least another six ships would have sunk or been seriously damaged if bombs had exploded; but the Argentine air forces paid a heavy price in plane and pilot losses.

388 Oakley, Derek. THE FALKLANDS MILITARY MACHINE. Tunbridge Wells: Spellmount, 1989, 192 pp.

Review of weapons and vehicles.

389 O'Ballance, Edgar. "The Other Falkland Campaign." MILITARY REVIEW, 63 (January 1983): 9–16.

On the role of the media in wartime; subjected to double censorship; no mention of SAS/SBS activities; sensational instance of "leak": claimed that the BBC announced 2 Para was prepared to attack at Goose Green on 28 May in time for Argentines to move in reinforcements; overall, the media was dissatisfied with the Ministry of Defence; on Argentine media, there was total censorship and outrageous claims of sinking and damaging British ships, especially the carriers and large transports.

390 Ogden, Chris. MAGGIE: AN INTIMATE PORTRAIT OF A WOMAN IN POWER. New York: Simon & Schuster, 1990, 384 pp.

By TIME magazine reporter; chapter 10 on "War in a Faraway Place" and 11 on "the Falklands Factor," pp. 178–99.

391 Osprey Publishing. MEN-AT-ARMS series. London: Osprey.

See Fowler [164], English [140], and Braybrook [59].

392 Pandolfe, Frank Craig. "South American Naval Development, 1965–1985: A Four Nation Study." Ph.D. diss., Fletcher School, Tufts, 1987.

Dissertation on naval developments in Brazil, Chile, Peru, and Argentina; about naval leaders, institutions, political power, and aspirations; naval power has been an important factor for 500 years; quantified naval acquisitions.

393 PARLIAMENTARY DEBATES. HANSARDS. House of Commons, 5th series, vols. 761-999; 6th series, vols. 1-81. London: HMSO, 1968–1985.

A standard source for many issues; see printed digest and summary on Falklands/Malvinas campaign, House of Commons [247].

394 PARLIAMENTARY DEBATES. House of Lords. London: HMSO 1982.

Not so important or as interesting as those of the House of Commons [393].

395 Parsons, Sir Anthony. "The Falklands Crisis in the United Nations, 31 March–14 June 1982." INTERNATIONAL AFFAIRS, 59 (Spring 1983): 169–78.

By the United Kingdom's permanent representative to the U.N.; noted the surprise of all concerned when the crisis broke; bilateral negotiations had been going on in New York; surprised at the extremely high level of interest in the crisis at the U.N.; recalled the super-human effort to gain passage of Resolution 502 of 3 April; meant reputation of Great Britain much enhanced.

396 Perkins, Roger. OPERATION PARAQUET: THE BATTLE FOR SOUTH GEORGIA. Chippenham: Picton, 1986, 272 pp.

A large picture book; some background; personal experiences and eyewitness accounts; details on the Davidoff affair; unprecedented public exposure on the operations of SAS and SBS; 22 SAS men were killed in a helicopter accident; no footnotes and no bibliography.

397 Perl, Raphael. THE FALKLANDS ISLAND DISPUTE IN INTERNATIONAL LAW AND POLITICS: A DOCUMENTARY SOURCEBOOK. New York and London: Oceana, 1983, 735 pp.

Included bibliography by E. Larson [310] with 196 entries; compilation of 52 documents involving treaties and other diplomatic papers.

398 Pernety, Antonie Joseph, ed. THE HISTORY OF A VOYAGE TO THE MALOUINE (OR FALKLAND) ISLANDS BY M. DE BOUGAINVILLE. 3 vols. London: Lister, 1769, 1770, 1787.

English and French editions.

399   Perrett, Bryan. WEAPONS OF THE FALKLANDS CONFLICT. New York: Sterling; Poole: Blandford, 1982, 1983, 152 pp.

Details on all ships and weapons, British and Argentine, including ELINT, SIGINT, and psychological warfare; illustrated.

400   Philippi, Alberto Jorge. "The Odyssey of a Skyhawk Pilot." NIProc, 109 (May 1983): 111-13.

By a captain, Argentine navy; about the Third Naval Attack Squadron, originally aboard the aircraft carrier but operated ashore during most of the campaign; determined that air-to-air combat with Harriers was too costly; began attacking shipping at height of 100 feet, then lowered to 50 feet; Philippi was shot down by a Harrier, rescued by ranch manager, and returned home.

401   Phipps, Colin. WHAT FUTURE FOR THE FALKLANDS? FABIAN TRACT # 450. London: Fabian Society, 1977, 16 pp.

An account of two Labour MPs, Phipps and John Gilbur, who went to the Falkland Islands in 1975, concluding that it was impossible to exploit economic potential without Argentine cooperation.

402   Pitt, Barrie. CORONEL AND FALKLANDS. American title: REVENGE AT SEA. New York: Stein & Day; London: Cassell, 1960, 1964, 191 pp.

A more recent account of the battles of 1914.

403   Planchar, R. LA GUERRE DE BOUT DU MONDE: ILES FALKLAND 1982. Paris: Denel, 1985.

A French account.

404   Plaschka, Richard G. MATROSEN, OFFIZIERE, REBELLEN: KRISENKONFRONTATIONEN ZUR SEE, 1900–1918. 2 vols. Vienna: Bohlaus, 1984, 774 pp.

By an academic, University of Vienna; to illustrate basic components of sea power using three naval battles as case studies, including Coronel/Falklands of 1914.

405   Pochhamer, Hans. BEFORE JUTLAND: ADMIRAL SPEE'S LAST VOYAGE: CORONEL AND THE BATTLE OF THE FALKLANDS. London: Jarrolds, 1931, 255 pp.

Translated by H. J. Stenning; recollections of a German officer prisoner.

406 Ponting, Clive. THE RIGHT TO KNOW: THE INSIDE STO-RY OF THE "BELGRANO" AFFAIR. London: Sphere, 1985, 214 pp.

About official secrecy; Ponting, a government bureaucrat between 1970 and 1984, was tried at Old Bailey for violating the Official Secrets Act, January 1985; claimed this was the most political trial of the twentieth century; details from his perspective on the sinking of BELGRANO; Ponting's accusations aimed at subsequent cover-up and misinformation by the government; on 11 February, found not guilty.

407 Ponting, Clive. SECRECY IN BRITAIN. HISTORICAL AS-SOCIATION STUDIES. Oxford: Blackwell, 1990, 96 pp.

An assessment of the control and flow of official information in Great Britain; noted some cases, especially his own associated with the BELGRANO sinking and subsequent sensational affair and trial for which he was acquitted.

408 Porter, Andrew and Stockwell, A. J. BRITISH IMPERIAL POLICY AND DECOLONIZATION, 1938–1964. Vol. I, 1938-1951. CAMBRIDGE COMMONWEALTH series. New York: St. Martins; London: Macmillan, 1987, 403 pp.

Background of colonialism and beginnings of decolonization.

409 Porter, Bernard. THE LION'S SHARE: A SHORT HISTORY OF BRITISH IMPERIALISM, 1850–1983. New York and London: Longman, 1975, 1984, 448 pp.

A history of modern colonialism based on economic, political, and social themes; economically determined but not the Marxist view; second edition incorporated Falklands/Malvinas campaign; British response based on nationalism, not imperialism; Falklands now seen as an even greater liability.

410 PORTSMOUTH NEWS. VICTORY IN THE FALKLANDS. PORTSMOUTH NEWS SPECIAL PUBLICATION. Portsmouth, July 1982, 24 pp.

Large magazine-type format; local perspectives and praise for British forces.

411   Preston, Antony. "EXOCET—The World's First Sea Skimmer." WARSHIP, 24 (1982): 275–81.
On surface-to-surface and other configurations of guided missiles, French designed in the late 1960s; "fire-and-forget" missile which has its own radar; 364-pound warhead.

412   Preston, Antony. HISTORY OF THE ROYAL NAVY IN THE TWENTIETH CENTURY. Novato, CA: Presidio; London: Bison, 1987, 224 pp.
From Edwardian navy through Falklands/Malvinas campaign, Falklands in chapter 9, pp. 190–205; colored illustrations.

413   Preston, Antony. SEA COMBAT OFF THE FALKLANDS. London: Willow, 1982, 143 pp.
Well-informed and authoritative account; "vital weakness" was gap in airborne early warning, impossible since the last attack carrier had been retired in 1978; informed details about aluminum superstructures, not prone to burn; virtually nothing on submarine operations.

414   Preston, Antony. "The West's Fighting Ships." Video. Tinley Park, IL: Fusion, n.d., 60 min.
Script by Preston, film footage on capabilities of Western navies.

415   Price, Alfred. HARRIER AT WAR. London: Allan, 1984, 120 pp.
Very large picture book; on "jump-jets"; in Falklands/Malvinas campaign, Harriers immediately established themselves as superior in air-to-air combat; used Sidewinder air-to-air infra-red homing missile; no air-to-air combat losses of Harriers.

416   Price, Alfred. INSTRUMENTS OF DARKNESS: THE HISTORY OF ELECTRONIC WARFARE. London: Kimber; London: Macdonald, 1967, 1977, 284 pp.
By RAF officer; reviewed history and uses of electronic warfare.

417   PROCEEDINGS OF THE NAVAL INSTITUTE. A monthly periodical. Annapolis, MD: NIP.
Maintained considerable coverage of the campaign.

418   Pugh, Philip G. "Maintenance of Post-War British Sea Power." WARSHIP, 35 (1986): 56–62.
Described the post-war transformation of the RN over the past 40 years.

419   Pym, Francis. "British Foreign Policy: Constraints and Opportunities." INTERNATIONAL AFFAIRS, 59 (Winter 1982–1983): 1-6.
Address at Chatham House by foreign secretary; general assessment.

420   Ramirez Mitchell, Ruben A. MALVINAS: SELECCION BIBLIOGRAFIA. Abstracts, 1983, 29 pp.
Abstracts of military bibliography on the Falklands/Malvinas.

421   Rasor, Eugene L. BRITISH NAVAL HISTORY SINCE 1815: A GUIDE TO THE LITERATURE. MILITARY HISTORY BIBLIOGRAPHIES series # 13. New York: Garland, 1990, 864 pp.
Over 3100 entries of publications since 1960; a historiographical survey including an extensive narrative section which integrated the entries; on the Falklands/Malvinas campaign, pp. 453–61.

422   Rattenbach, Benjamin. RATTENBACH REPORT. Rattenbach Commission. Buenos Aires: Siete Dias, 1983.
By Argentine general as an official investigation of the war; kept secret but excerpts leaked; commission headed by Commodore R. O. Moro [367].

423   Ravenal, Eugenio A. L. ISLES OF DISCORD: A FILE ON THE FALKLANDS (MALVINAS). Geneva: Siboney & Ventura, 1983, 189 pp.
On the earliest history of the dispute; quoted Patrick Henry: "We must fight!"; blurb claimed it was a dispassionate look at the historical and legal background.

424   Record, Jeffrey. "The Falklands War." WASHINGTON QUARTERLY, 5 (Autumn 1982): 43–51.
Noted military lessons from the campaign.

425   Rees, Wyn. "The 1957 Sandys White Paper: New Priorities in British Defence Policy?" JOURNAL OF STRATEGIC STUDIES, 12 (June 1989): 215–29.

From Duncan Sandys in the Harold Macmillan government, "Outline of Future Policy" incorporated significant cuts in all armed forces after the Suez fiasco; maintained the nuclear capability.

426 Regan, Geoffrey. SOMEONE HAD BLUNDERED: A HISTORICAL SURVEY OF MILITARY INCOMPETENCE. London: Batsford, 1987, 320 pp.
Series of case studies of incompetence, blunders, and insufficiencies; RN cited in six cases such as Singapore, Suez, and failure to implement convoy.

427 Reginald, Robert and Elliot, Jeffrey M. TEMPEST IN A TEAPOT: THE FALKLAND ISLANDS WAR. San Bernardino, CA: Borgo, 1983, 176 pp.
Recalled gunboat diplomacy and European imperialism; aimed to present both sides of "this bizarre little war"; consistently used tea analogy; several errors.

428 Reimann, Elisabeth. LAS MALVINAS TRAICION: MADE IN USA. Mexico City: Ediciones el Caballito, 1983, 142 pp.
Recalled the Monroe Doctrine and U.S. interventions.

429 "Report on the Falklands." AVIATION WEEK AND SPACE TECHNOLOGY, 117 (19 July and 26 July 1982): 18–22 and 24–25.
Samples of coverage by this popular, authoritative weekly; reported British use of chaff as countermeasure to EXOCET missile attacks, but something went wrong when ATLANTIC CONVEYOR was hit; GLAMORGAN hit by land-based EXOCET; details on performance of other weapons.

430 Richelson, Jeffrey and Ball, Desmond. THE TIES THAT BIND: INTELLIGENCE COOPERATION BETWEEN THE UK-USA COUNTRIES. London: Allen & Unwin, 1986, 420 pp.
Recounted a cooperative endeavor, an "intelligence club," of Great Britain, the U.S., Australia, New Zealand, and Canada during and after World War II.

431 Ridlon, David. "Shots in the Dark: British Tactical Intelligence in the Falklands War." MILITARY INTELLIGENCE, 15 (July-September 1989): 40–49.

By captain, U.S. army; noted British use of extensive patrolling for tactical intelligence, particularly by special forces put ashore on the islands and, in one case, on the mainland; also the use of the "phantom voice," Falklands resident Reginald Silvey, an amateur radio operator who reported events and disrupted Argentine communications.

432 Rippy, James Frederick. BRITISH INVESTMENTS IN LATIN AMERICA, 1822–1949: A CASE STUDY IN THE OPERATIONS OF PRIVATE ENTERPRISE IN RETARDED REGIONS. Minneapolis: U Minnesota P; Hamden: Archon, 1959, 1966, 256 pp.
British overseas investments peaked in the 1920s; on Argentina, pp. ʾ59–70.

433 Rock, David. ARGENTINA, 1516–1982: FROM SPANISH COLONIZATION TO THE FALKLANDS WAR. Berkeley: U California P, 1985, 1987, 505 pp.
A comprehensive and intelligent history; on the campaign, pp. 375–76.

434 Rojas, Gralalberto A. Muller. LAS MALVINAS: TRAGICOMEDIA EN TRES ACTOS. Caracas: Ensayo Serie Menor, 1983, 304 pp.
On the war as tragicomedy from the Argentine perspective.

435 Romero Briasco, Jesus and Mafe Huertas, Salvador. FALKLANDS, WITNESS OF BATTLES. Valencia: Federico Domenech, 1984, 1985, 253 pp.
Large picture book; history of the air war, British and Argentine; operations and damage demonstrated.

436 Roth, Roberto. DESPUES DE MALVINAS, QUE . . . ? Buenos Aires: Ediciones La Campana, 1982, 165 pp.
A devastating critique of the war, "an obscene parody of patriotism"; courageous, forceful, candid; compliments to the air force where there were no "fat brigadiers," but contempt for the navy and army.

437 Rouquie, Alain. "Argentina: The Departure of the Military—End of a Political Cycle or Just Another Episode?" INTERNATIONAL AFFAIRS, 59 (Autumn 1983): 575–86.

From a Paris think-tank; another cycle of military rule coming to an end with the usual economic catastrophe, and, in this case, the tragic adventure in the South Atlantic; accused the U.S. of treachery.

438 Royal Institute of International Affairs. THE FALKLAND ISLANDS DISPUTE: INTERNATIONAL DIMENSIONS. London: RIIA, 1982.
A think-tank assessment while the campaign was still going on; general pessimism and distaste for the military option.

439 Royle, Trevor. WAR REPORT: THE WAR CORRESPON-DENT'S VIEW OF BATTLE FROM THE CRIMEA TO THE FALK-LANDS. Edinburgh: Mainstream, 1987, 240 pp.
A history of the war correspondent; for Falklands/Malvinas campaign, pp. 216–25; described experiences of journalists of the task force; RN completely unprepared to deal with the media; problems created by arm-chair strategists; cited Max Hastings, Robert Harris, Robert Fox, and Brian Hanrahan as outstanding examples; the campaign increased interest in the media: GUARDIAN sales were up by 50,000; ITN News audience up 20%.

440 Royal United Services Institute for Defence Studies. RUSI AND BRASSEY'S DEFENCE YEARBOOK, 1984. New York and Oxford: Brassey's, 1984, 429 pp.
94th year, annual; series of articles, several on the aftermath of the campaign.

441 RUSI JOURNAL SPECIAL SUPPLEMENT. "The Military Helicopter: Future Operations and Developments." RUSI, 134 (Winter 1989): 1-36.
All about the Allied development, deployment, use, and future of helicopters; nothing strictly on use in the Falklands/Malvinas.

442 Samuel, Raphael, ed. PATRIOTISM: THE MAKING AND UNMAKING OF BRITISH NATIONAL IDENTITY. HISTORY WORKSHOP symposium. 3 vols. New York: Routledge, 1989, 944 pp.
Series of essays from a symposium sponsored by the History Workshop; study of patriotism originating from opposition to

the Falklands/Malvinas campaign; failure of anti-war movement; country response was militaristic, excessive rhetoric, and ironic; a naval force barely scraped together cheered as it went off to fight a Third World power.

443 Sanders, David, Ward, Hugh, and Marsh, David. "Government Popularity and the Falklands War: A Reassessment." BRITISH JOURNAL OF POLITICAL SCIENCE, 17 (1987); 281-313.

Debate over "Falklands factor"; claimed it has been "substantially overestimated"; many charts and statistics used to prove that the government popularity was due to improved macroeconomic management; see H. Clarke [95] for opposing view.

444 Scheina, Robert L. "Argentina's Navy in the Falklands War." JANE'S NAVAL REVIEW, 1983–1984 (1983): 21-27.

From interviews with over 50 naval and marine officers; concluded that the invasion plan was tied to the scrap-metal actions; plans were developed in February and March 1982.

445 Scheina, Robert L. LATIN AMERICA: A NAVAL HISTORY, 1810–1987. Annapolis: NIP, 1987, 467 pp.

Extensively researched; the most comprehensive account of this approach to Latin American history; two chapters on the Falklands/Malvinas campaign, pp. 234–92, and appendix, pp. 333–42; claimed Argentine naval performance was "first rate" and the defeat was due to faulty equipment and lack of supplies.

446 Scheina, Robert L. "Latin American Navies." NIProc, 109 (March 1983): 30–34.

Lessons for South American navies from the Falklands/Malvinas campaign; Argentina was acutely vulnerable to the arms embargo; serious gaps in submarine and anti-submarine warfare; the Argentine navy did remain intact, the Marine Corps performed well, and naval aviators were innovative in adapting EXOCET for use against British warships.

447 Scheina, Robert L. "The Malvinas Campaign." NIProc, 109 (May 1983): 98–117.

By American Coast Guard historian; much research in Latin America; the Argentine initiative to invade was not to distract from other problems but because of years of frustration; details on self-training and installation of EXOCETs by naval aviators.

448 Scheina, Robert L. "Super Etendard; Super Squadron." NIProc, 109 (March 1983): 135–36.
Naval Second Attack Squadron obtained Super Etendards and EXOCETs; adapted and installed them themselves; in 1979, had ordered 14 aircraft, 5 had arrived, used 4; none were lost during the campaign; illustrations.

449 Scheina, Robert L. "Where Were Those Argentine Subs?" NIProc, 110 (March 1984): 115–20.
Interviews with submariners; noted that SAN LUIS did attack British forces, e.g., torpedoes were fired at frigates on 10 May but the fire control system was in manual and the periscope was not used; all missed; SANTA FE was disabled by a helicopter at South Georgia.

450 Schonfeld, Manfred. LA GUERRA AUSTRAL: ARTICULOS PUBLICADOS EN EL DIARIO LA PRENSA DE BUENOS AIRES. Buenos Aires: Desafios Editores, 1982, 382 pp.
Preface by Victor A. Guerrero Leconte; collection of articles written for LA PRENSA; heavily biased; recovery of Malvinas was "a national destiny."

451 Seymour, William. BRITISH SPECIAL FORCES. London: Sidgwick & Jackson, 1985, 358 pp.
Foreword by David Stirling; details on the wartime exploits of British special forces; for the Falklands/Malvinas, pp. 303–17; retaking South Georgia.

452 Shackleton, Lord. ECONOMIC SURVEY OF THE FALKLAND ISLANDS. 2 vols. London: Economist Intelligence Unit, 1976.
The much publicized "SHACKLETON I" Report; extensive economic survey to determine the potential for development; conclusions were not encouraging.

453 Shackleton, Lord. FALKLAND ISLANDS: ECONOMIC STUDY, 1982. Cmnd 8653. London: HMSO, September 1982.
"SHACKLETON II" Report; a second study made after the campaign; concluded that the dispute over sovereignty constrained potential for economic development.

172   The Falklands/Malvinas Campaign

454   Sherrard, D. G. TO ANTARCTICA WITH THE ROYAL
NAVY. New York: Vantage, 1980, 1981, 132 pp.
Account of one of the annual voyages, filled with interesting
sidelights such as exotic ports and naval lore.

455   SIETE DIAS ILUATRADOS. A weekly review. Buenos Aires.
Book, drama, and film reviews.

456   Skidelsky, Robert J. A. THATCHERISM. London: Chatto &
Windus, 1988, 214 pp.
Series of lectures, University of Warwick, 1988; nothing speci-
fically on Falklands/Malvinas campaign.

457   Smith, Dan. THE DEFENCE OF THE REALM IN THE
1980s. London: Croom Helm, 1980, 276 pp.
General survey of all of the forces, NATO, costs, technology,
arms control, and nuclear capability.

458   Smith, David and Wynn, Andrew. HMS "ARK ROYAL":
THE SHIP AND HER MEN. Liskeard: Maritime, 1989, 80 pp.
By officer, RN; on the light carrier completed after the cam-
paign.

459   Smith, John. 74 DAYS: AN ISLANDER'S DIARY OF THE
FALKLANDS OCCUPATION. London: Century, 1984, 255 pp.
Foreword consisted of statements of Margaret Thatcher; by
employee of British Antarctic Survey, resident for 25 years; to
convey the enormity of the events of 1982; obvious resentment
over each of the series of concessions to Argentina in the decades
before 1982.

460   Smith, R. G. [Cover Picture]. Art. NIProc, 109 (May 1983):
cover.
Exciting, colorful, double-page fold-out picture of two Type
21 frigates in "Bomb Alley" being attacked by four A-4s on 21
May; ARDENT and two A-4s lost in the attack; prints cost $45.00,
available from N. B. Fine Arts, Torrance, CA.

461   Snyder, William P. THE POLITICS OF BRITISH DEFENSE
POLICY, 1945–1962. Columbus: Ohio State UP, 1964, 1965, 296
pp.

By an American scholar from a Princeton dissertation [462]; analysis of the effort to balance domestic capacities and international commitments; a case study of a state increasingly incapable of manipulating its international environment; the culmination was the Suez crisis of 1956; this situation was the background for the dilemma faced by the government in 1982.

462 Snyder, William P. "The Politics of British Defense Policy, 1951-1961." Ph.D. diss., Princeton, 1963, 419 pp.
The dissertation which was the basis for the analysis above [461].

463 Socarras, Michael P. "The Argentine Invasion of the Falklands and International Norms of Signalling." YALE JOURNAL OF INTERNATIONAL LAW, 10 (1985).
A professional analysis based on international law.

464 Soriano, Osvaldo. A FUNNY DIRTY LITTLE WAR. Barcelona: Bruguera; New York: Readers International, 1980, 1983, 1986, 108 pp.
Translated by Nick Caistor; by an Argentine writer opposed to the government; originally published in Barcelona; set in a sleepy little town featuring Peronist henchmen and municipal corruption; upset the Peronists and the military Junta.

465 Soriano, Osvaldo. NO HABRA MAS PENAS NI OLVIDO. Barcelona: Bruguera; Buenos Aires: Sudamericana, 1980, 1983, 1986, 108 pp.
Original Spanish edition of [464].

466 Southby-Tailyour, Ewen. FALKLAND ISLANDS SHORES. London: Conway, 1985.
The much acclaimed and detailed geographical-nautical survey of the waters and shores of the Falkland/Malvinas Islands conducted by this Royal Marine officer who completed it while assigned to the Marine Guard there several years before; Southby-Tailyour was a yachting expert and was called in to assist in the planning and executing of the counter-invasion; an incredibly useful document for the purposes of intelligence and planning.

467 Speed, Keith. SEA CHANGE: THE BATTLE FOR THE FALKLANDS AND THE FUTURE OF BRITAIN'S NAVY. Bath: Ashgrove, 1982, 194 pp.

Written shortly after he was fired as first lord of the Admiralty—he being the last holder of that office because it was never revived; he was fired for openly objecting to the 1981 White Paper (Nott) cutbacks; an extraordinary memoir, extremely candid and lacking in rancor; recounted information about the Falklands/Malvinas in the 1970s and 1980s.

468 Spencer-Cooper, Henry. THE BATTLE OF THE FALKLAND ISLANDS: BEFORE AND AFTER. New York and London: Cassell, 1919, 236 pp.
An account written shortly after the war was over.

469 Stanford, Peter. "Britain's Surface Navy—Whither Away?" NIProc, 115 (January 1989): 44–48.
Presented yet another example of the value of maintaining a high level of preparation of surface warfare forces, in this case, the Persian Gulf crisis of the late 1980s; lamented the fact that promised numbers of destroyer-types were not forthcoming.

470 Stewart, Norma Kinzer. SOUTH ATLANTIC CONFLICT OF 1982: A CASE STUDY IN MILITARY COHESION. RESEARCH REPORT # 1469. Washington: U.S. Army Research Institute, April 1988.
An analysis by this official think-tank.

471 Stockholm International Peace Research Institute. THE FALKLANDS/MALVINAS CONFLICT. Stockholm: SIPRI, 1983.
An analysis by this prestigious international think-tank.

472 Strachan, Hew. "The British Way in Warfare Revisited." HISTORICAL JOURNAL, 26 (September 1983): 447–61.
A review essay on military history in Great Britain; focused on four historians: Sir Michael Howard, Paul Kennedy, John Terraine, and Correlli Barnett; assessed their writings on sea power, land warfare, strategy, geopolitics, limited war, and submarine warfare; conclusions stressed interdependence of maritime and continental, sea and land, roles in warfare.

473 Strange, Ian J. THE FALKLAND ISLANDS. Newton Abbot: David & Charles, 1972, 1981, 1983, 328 pp.
Updated editions; on geographic features, administration, economic development, and post-war rehabilitation.

474 Strange, Ian J. THE FALKLANDS: SOUTH ATLANTIC IS-LANDS. New York: Dodd, Mead, 1985, 160 pp.

By an agricultural expert who set up an experimental farm; observations about geography, nature, wildlife, farming, and the Kelpers.

475 Sturtivant, Ray. BRITISH NAVAL AVIATION: THE FLEET AIR ARM, 1917–1990. Annapolis: NIP; London: Arms & Armour, 1990, 224 pp.

160 illustrations; naval aviation originated about 1910; on Falklands/Malvinas campaign, pp. 203–9.

476 SUNDAY EXPRESS MAGAZINE TEAM. WAR IN THE FALKLANDS: THE CAMPAIGN IN PICTURES. London: Weidenfeld & Nicolson, 1982, 160 pp.

Introduction by Ron Hall; magazine format with hard cover; outstanding collection of photographs.

477 Taylor, A.J.P. AN OLD MAN'S DIARY. London: Hamilton, 1984, 163 pp.

A collection of articles and reviews from this most eminent of historians; in "passing comments" he said, "I regret only one entry. That was my first reaction to the Argentine invasion." He then apologized for supporting the war and noted that his next entry opposed the war "as firmly as Dr. Johnson had condemned a similar war some 200 years before" (p. vii); see Johnson [275].

478 Taylor, J.P. "Argentina: The Falklands and Colonialism." ATLANTIC, 250 (August 1982): 22–26.

By an anthropologist from Rice University who had previously lived in Argentina and in Great Britain.

479 Terzano, Daniel. 5000 ADIOSES A PUERTO ARGENTINO. Buenos Aires: Editorial Galerna, 1985, 180 pp.

An account of the Argentine occupation.

480 Thompson, Julian. NO PICNIC: 3 COMMANDO BRIGADE IN THE SOUTH ATLANTIC, 1982. London: Secker & Warburg, 1985, 219 pp.

By Royal Marine officer, the commander of 3 Commando; recounted operations at South Georgia, Goose Green, "yomping" east, and Port Stanley, all of which were "no picnic"; noted that at all times they were outnumbered and that their success was dependent on professionalism, experience, training, and persistence; of interest to similar military professionals.

481 Thornton, A. P. IMPERIALISM IN THE TWENTIETH CENTURY. Minneapolis: U Minnesota P, 1977, 1978, 375 pp.
Balanced assessment by an experienced historian, University of Toronto; covered the philosophical and ideological debate and included Europe, the U.S., and Japan.

482 Till, Geoffrey, ed. BRITAIN AND NATO'S NORTHERN FLANK. New York: St. Martins; London: Macmillan, 1988, 224 pp.
Edited by a professor, Kings College, London, and Royal Naval College, Greenwich; a series of essays focusing on an important commitment of British forces associated with NATO.

483 Till, Geoffrey, ed. THE FUTURE OF BRITISH POWER. London: Macmillan, 1984, 281 pp.
36 essays for a conference, Kings College, London, and Royal Naval College, Greenwich, November 1983; by the most eminent observers including high government officials on the present and future of maritime matters for Great Britain.

484 Till, Geoffrey, ed. MARITIME STRATEGY AND THE NUCLEAR AGE. New York: St. Martins, 1982, 1984, 305 pp.
A series of essays by eminent experts including Stephen Roskill, Bryan Ranft, John Hattendorf, and Barry Hunt; second edition incorporated assessment of Falklands/Malvinas campaign, pp. 239–56, "the world's most serious naval war for nearly 40 years" (p. 239); both sides were guilty of underestimation; it was a limited war with limited means, a concept advocated by the great naval theorist, Sir Julian Corbett.

485 Till, Geoffrey. MODERN SEA POWER: AN INTRODUCTION. Washington and London: Brassey's, 1987, 195 pp.
Excellent illustrations; emphasis on the impact of technology such as nuclear power, nuclear weapons, and electronics.

486 TIME weekly newsmagazine. New York.
Devoted five cover stories to the Falklands/Malvinas campaign between 19 April and 7 June 1982.

487 Tinker, David. MALVINAS: CARTAS DE UN MARINO INGLES. Buenos Aires: Emece Editores, 1983, 214 pp.
Spanish translation of [488].

488 Tinker, David. A MESSAGE FROM THE FALKLANDS: THE LIFE AND GALLANT DEATH OF DAVID TINKER, LIEUTENANT, RN. New York: Penguin, 1982, 1983, 214 pp.
Compiled by the father, Hugh Tinker; a poignant tale of maturation and of growing opposition to the war; Tinker, a naval officer since 1975, aboard GLAMORGAN, and killed when his ship was hit by an EXOCET; an example of front-line eloquence in poetry and prose; father and son obviously developed increasing doubts about the conflict, concluding finally that it was solely for the politicians, especially the "dictators," Thatcher and Nott; foresaw a future "Fortress Falklands."

489 Tinker, Hugh. "The Falklands after Three Years." ROUND TABLE, 296 (October 1985): 339–44.
The father of the above [488]; "Thoughts aroused by the service at St. Paul's, 14 June 1985," the third-year commemoration service; still concluding that the war was all politics and a waste.

490 TLS: TIMES LITERARY SUPPLEMENT. A weekly review. London.
Timely reviews and commentary.

491 Train, Harry D. "An Analysis of the Falkland/Malvinas Islands Campaign." NWCR, 41 (Winter 1988): 33–50.
By an admiral, U.S. Navy; the campaign was a classic case of the breakdown of deterrence and should not have occurred; first use of modern cruise missiles, nuclear-powered attack submarines, and VSTOL aircraft; the large number of unexploded bombs could have greatly increased British losses; details on factors influencing selection of the landing site at San Carlos.

492 Tracy, Nicholas. "The Falkland Islands Crisis of 1770: Use of Naval Force." ENGLISH HISTORICAL REVIEW, 90 (January 1975): 40–75.
By a Nova Scotian; incident in which Britain and Bourbon France-Spain almost went to war; a British captain forced the Spanish to withdraw from the Falklands/Malvinas; the French later sold their claim to Spain.

493 Treverton, Gregory and Lippincott, Don. FALKLANDS/ MALVINAS. Pittsburgh: Pew Program, 1988.
An assessment for the Pew Program; similar to a think-tank.

494 Troiani, Osiris. OPERACION MALVINAS I: MARTINEZ DE HOZ EN LONDRES. Buenos Aires: El Cid Editor, 1982, 112 pp.
Published in April 1982; a review of diplomatic preliminaries, the SHACKLETON REPORT [452], and various models for a diplomatic solution.

495 Turner, Stansfield. "The Unobvious Lessons of the Falklands War." NIProc, 109 (April 1983): 50–57.
By an American admiral and former head of the CIA; stressed mostly political lessons; lack of foresight meant nations were dragged into an unnecessary war.

496 Turolo, Carlos M. ASI LUCHARON. Buenos Aires: Sudamericana, 1982, 1983, 327 pp.
A semi-official view of the campaign from the perspective of the Argentine army.

497 Turolo, Carlos M., ed. MALVINAS: TESTIMONIO DE SU GOBERNADOR. Buenos Aires: Sudamericana, 337 pp.
A lengthy interview with the military governor of the occupied Malvinas, General Mario B. Menendez; an apology and explanation; he learned about the plan in March, but then the date was accelerated to April; claimed he was not fully informed about the changing situation and that his proposals were often ignored.

498 Tustin, W. J. "The Logistics of the Falklands War." 2 parts. AQDJ, 114 (1984): 295–301, 399–411.
Description of British logistics from preparation for the task force to arrival in Port Stanley; details on STUFT and on moving major equipment and supplies by trail, road, sea, and air; on the use of Ascension Island as a base; on the amphibious landings, which, he contended, were a complete surprise; outlined logistical problems.

499 Underwood, Geoffrey. OUR FALKLANDS WAR: THE MEN OF THE TASK FORCE TELL THEIR STORY. London: Maritime, 1983, 144 pp.

Introduction by General Sir Jeremy Moore; slick, illustrated format; interviews with participants including the commanding officer of HMS CONQUEROR and the amphibious coordinator.

500 United Kingdom. Central Office of Information. BRITAIN AND THE FALKLANDS ISLANDS: A DOCUMENTARY RECORD. London: HMSO, 1982, 96 pp.
An official report.

501 United Kingdom. Central Office of Information. THE FALKLANDS ISLANDS AND DEPENDENCIES. London: HMSO, March 1982, 8 pp.
An informative pamphlet.

502 United Kingdom. Central Office of Information. BRITAIN AND THE LATIN AMERICAN INDEPENDENCE MOVEMENTS. London: HMSO, September 1982.
A report reviewing the British position in past independence movements.

503 United Kingdom. Foreign and Commonwealth Office. ARGENTINE MISINFORMATION: BACKGROUND BRIEFING. London: HMSO, July 1982.
An official effort to counteract what was claimed to be a large-scale propaganda campaign.

504 United Kingdom. Foreign and Commonwealth Office. THE DISPUTED ISLANDS: THE FALKLANDS CRISIS: A HISTORY. London: HMSO, 1982.
A review of essential diplomatic positions.

505 United Kingdom. Foreign and Commonwealth Office. THE FALKLAND ISLANDS: THE FACTS. London: HMSO, 1982, 11 pp.
A pamphlet presenting mostly statistics.

506 United Kingdom. Foreign and Commonwealth Office. THE FALKLAND ISLANDS: NEGOTIATIONS FOR A PEACEFUL SETTLEMENT. WHITE PAPER. London, HMSO, 20 May 1982.
A progress report of efforts at a negotiated settlement.

507 Van Sant Hall, Marshall. ARGENTINE POLICY IN THE FALKLANDS WAR: THE POLITICAL RESULTS. Newport, RI: U.S. Naval War College, 25 June 1983.

An assessment for war college use.

508 Vaux, Nick F. MARCH TO THE SOUTH ATLANTIC: 42 COMMANDO IN THE FALKLANDS. London: Buchan & Enright, 1986, 260 pp.
By a general, Royal Marines, commanding officer of 42 Commandos; recounted operations and experiences of the land war.

509 Vaux, Nick F. TAKE THAT HILL! ROYAL MARINES IN THE FALKLANDS WAR. Washington: Pergamon-Brassey, 1986, 1987, 256 pp.
Forewords by Max Hastings and General P. X. Kelly; the story of 650 members of 42 Commandos; individual exploits; nothing on grand strategy.

510 Villar, Roger. MERCHANT SHIPS AT WAR: THE FALKLANDS EXPERIENCE. Annapolis: NIP; London: Conway, 1984, 192 pp.
By a captain, RN; the story of STUFT; the process of planning, mobilizing, altering, and sailing of a huge, diverse group of over 50 merchant ships of all types to participate in wartime operations 8,000 miles from a regular base; examples of alterations and modifications included helicopter decks, communications equipment, weapons, decoys, distilling plants, and electronic facilities.

511 Villar, Roger. "Merchant Ships at War: The Falklands Experience." WARSHIP, 29 (1984): 2–8.
An article describing STUFT; see book [510].

512 Viola, Oscar Luis. LA DERROTA DIPLOMATICA Y MILITAR: CAUSAS PERSPECTIVAS SOLUCIONES. Buenos Aires: Tinta Dueva, 1983.
A review of various aspects of the conflict and some possible solutions.

513 Wain, Christopher. "The Aftermath of War: How the Journalists Saw the Falklands Campaign." THE LISTENER (3 March 1983): 20–21.
A review of the literature about the campaign; the first "history" appeared one week before the Argentine surrender!; assessed such accounts as those of Max Hastings and Simon Jenkins [229],

the SUNDAY TIMES Insight Team [137], Robert Fox [166], David Tinker [488], and Tam Dalyell [115, 116, 117].

514 Wallace, William. "How Frank Was Franks?" INTERNATIONAL AFFAIRS, 59 (Summer 1983): 453–58.
An appraisal of the FRANKS REPORT [168], the most extensive investigation of the campaign, in this case, events leading up to the Argentine invasion; seen as "an extraordinary document" in that it exonerated the government but included numerous indictments in the text; reviewed a succession of "signals" from 1977–1982 which could have been read by Argentina as evidence of diminishing British interest; noted that the Falklands Lobby was uniformly hostile to efforts at solution but that a majority of the Kelpers were undecided; that Parliament had given in to the pressures of the lobby and then permitted drift subsequently.

515 Wapshott, Nicholas and Brock, George. THATCHER. London: Futura; London: Macdonald, 1983, 295 pp.
A review of the first term of office as prime minister, 1979–1983.

516 Warner, Philip. THE SPECIAL BOAT SQUADRON. London: Sphere, 1983, 150 pp.
Popularized and superficial; excessive errors.

517 Watson, Bruce W. and Dunn, Peter M., eds. MILITARY LESSONS OF THE FALKLANDS WAR: VIEWS FROM THE UNITED STATES. Boulder, CO: Westview; London: Arms & Armour, 1984, 196 pp.
Foreword by F. Clifton Berry; an analysis of the campaign by U.S. experts; noted that Argentina blamed the U.S. for excessive assistance to Britain and Britain blamed the U.S. for insufficient assistance; claimed that Russia offered Argentina intelligence information but the effort at communications hook-up failed; claimed that Peru, Israel, and Libya did provide military assistance to Argentina.

518 Way, Peter, ed. THE FALKLANDS WAR. London: Marshall Cavendish, 1983.
An assessment of the campaign.

519 Webb, Robert K. MODERN ENGLAND: FROM THE EIGHTEENTH CENTURY TO THE PRESENT. New York: Harper & Row, 1968, 1980, 685 pp.

An excellent synthesis of modern British history.

520   Weber, Hermann. "FALKLAND-ISLANDS" ODER "MAL-VINAS?": DER STATUS DER FALKLANDINSELN IM STREIT ZWISCHEN GROSSBRITANNIEN UN ARGENTINIEN ["FALK-LANDS" OR "MALVINAS?": THE STATUS OF THE FALK-LAND ISLANDS IN THE DISPUTE BETWEEN GREAT BRITAIN AND ARGENTINA]. Frankfurt on Main: Metzner, 1977, 193 pp.
A German assessment.

521   Weinberger, Caspar. FIGHTING FOR PEACE: SEVEN CRITICAL YEARS IN THE PENTAGON. New York: Warner; London: Joseph, 1990, 464 pp.
Memoirs of the U.S. secretary of defense during the campaign; on Falklands/Malvinas campaign, pp. 203–18; immediately demonstrated initiatives in fulfilling all needs requested by the British, e.g., aircraft fuel, Sidewinder air-to-air missiles, and intelligence facilities; "My role was assistant supply sergeant" (p. 203).

522   Wettern, Desmond. THE DECLINE OF BRITISH SEAPOWER. London: Jane's, 1982, 462 pp.
By a journalist; a chronological survey of the reduction in size of the RN; not scholarly, poorly organized.

523   WEYER'S WARSHIPS OF THE WORLD. Annual editions. Baltimore: Nautical Aviation; London: Weyer, various, c. 750 pp.
German and English editions; an informative reference guide and naval annual; scale drawings of every ship in every navy of the world; included naval aircraft and missiles.

524   "Who Killed Hilda Murrell?" A Play. May 1986.
Presented at Tricycle Theatre, London; author unknown; a consequence of the Clive Ponting affair, 1984–1986; Hilda Murrell was the 78-year-old aunt of an intelligence official and she died or was killed while authorities searched her home for evidence.

525   Williams, Glyn and Ramsden, John. RULING BRITANNIA: A POLITICAL HISTORY OF BRITAIN, 1688–1988. New York and London: Longman, 1990, 1991, 559 pp.
A recent textbook; on Falklands/Malvinas campaign, pp. 105, 454–45, 493; noted quite unexpected resurgence of patriotism

including some violent manifestations in the popular press.

526 Williams, Phil. "Miscalculations, Crisis Management and the Falklands Conflict." WORLD TODAY, 39 (April 1983): 144–49.

An aspect of the "signals" controversy; Great Britain contributed to the miscalculations because of the withdrawal of ENDURANCE and by an unwillingness to compromise; concluded that the basic conditions for crisis management were not met.

527 Williams, Ray. ROYAL NAVY AIRCRAFT SINCE 1945. Annapolis: NIP, 1989, 184 pp.

A history of the post–World War II fleet aircraft, including 44 aircraft types.

528 Windsor, Philip. "Diplomatic Dimensions of the Falklands Crisis." MILLENNIUM, 12 (Spring 1983): 88–96.

A survey of diplomatic issues.

529 Winton, John. AIR POWER AT SEA: 1945 TO TODAY. New York: Carroll & Graf; London: Sidgwick & Jackson, 1987, 192 pp.

By a prolific military-naval historian; on post–World War II carrier operations; on Falklands/Malvinas campaign, pp. 140–77.

530 Wood, Derek and Hewish, Mark. "The Falklands Conflict." 3 parts. INTERNATIONAL DEFENCE REVIEW, 15 (1982–1983): various.

Series of articles on air operations, missile performance, and naval operations.

531 Woods, John E. "The Royal Navy since World War II." NIProc, 108 (March 1982): 82–90.

The story of decline; in 1945 there were 990 combat units in the RN, by 1952 it was down to 123; various defence reviews further reduced the forces.

532 Woolf, Cecil and Moorcroft, Jean. AUTHORS TAKE SIDES ON THE FALKLANDS: TWO QUESTIONS ON THE FALKLANDS CONFLICT ANSWERED BY MORE THAN A HUNDRED MAINLY BRITISH AUTHORS. London: Cecil Woolf, 1982, 144 pp.

An unsuccessful effort to survey an important segment of society; unable to synthesize.

533 Wyllie, James H. THE INFLUENCE OF BRITISH ARMS: AN ANALYSIS OF BRITISH MILITARY INTERVENTION SINCE 1956. Winchester, MA: Allen & Unwin, 1984, 137 pp.

A survey of British military interventions after the Suez crisis: e.g., Oman, Jordan, Kuwait, Cyprus, Malaysia, and, most recently, the Falklands/Malvinas, which was not intervention, but liberation; concluded that these types of operations should be left to the U.S. (!).

534 Young, Elizabeth. "Falklands Fall-out: Note of the Month." WORLD TODAY, 38 (September 1982): 327–30.

A reaction to various writings on the campaign.

535 Young, Hugo. THE IRON LADY: A BIOGRAPHY OF MARGARET THATCHER. New York: Farrar & Strauss Giroux; New York: Hill & Wang, 1989, 1990, 581 pp.

The title was originally a Soviet dubbing of the then leader of the Conservative party; on Falklands/Malvinas campaign, pp. 247–92; concluded "Falklands factor" guaranteed a Conservative triumph at the next election.

536 Young, Hugo. ONE OF US. London: Macmillan, 1989.

By a well-known journalist; a detailed biography of Thatcher.

537 Young, Hugo and Sloman, Anne. THE THATCHER PHENOMENON. London: BBC, 1986, 144 pp.

The narrative for a series of BBC-Radio documentaries; involved 60 interviews.

ADDENDUM

538 Andrews, James. CANCELLATIONS OF THE FALKLAND ISLANDS AND DEPENDENCIES AND THE HANDSTRUCK STAMPS. London: Robson Lowe, 1956, 56 pp.

Foreword by B.S.H. Grant; companion to B.S.H. Grant [205]; elaboration about the unique characteristics of Philatelic factors associated with the Falkland Islands; authors mentioned are fellows of the Royal Philatelic Society.

539 Arthur, Max. MEN OF THE RED BERET: AIRBORNE FORCES, 1940–1990. London: Hutchinson, 1990, 430 pp.
Oral history approach, not a history of these commando-type forces; "to capture the spirit" of the actions of these special units, including the Falklands/Malvinas campaign.

540 Barnes, Robert F. POSTAL CANCELLATIONS OF THE FALKLAND ISLANDS. London: n.p., 1982, 144 pp.
Focused on the most important feature which made the Falkland Islands so unique in the Philatelic factor.

541 Beaver, Paul. BRITISH NAVAL AIR POWER, 1945 TO THE PRESENT. WARBIRDS ILLUSTRATED series #33. London: Arms and Armour; New York: Sterling, 1985, 67 pp.
Beaver has formulated several of these detailed surveys and histories of various armed forces, in this case, aspects of British naval aviation contributions and exploits after World War II; profusely illustrated with detailed captions.

542 Beck, Peter J. "The Conflict Potential of the 'Dots on the Map.' " INTERNATIONAL HISTORY REVIEW, 13 (February 1991): 124–33.
Review article including Dillon [129] and Freedman [175], both being recent and mature analytical syntheses of the campaign and its consequences; there was general praise for both; noted that the Falklands/Malvinas question was #242 on the priority listing of the British foreign office; that Dillon [129] indicted the Thatcher government for negligence and incompetence prior to the Argentine invasion especially in the categories of negotiation, intelligence, and political coordination; noted that the Argentine foreign minister Costa Mendez has suspended plans to publish his memoirs; concluded that the primary loser in the Falklands/Malvinas imbroglio was the United States.

543 Bywater, Hector C. CRUISERS IN BATTLE: NAVAL "LIGHT CAVALRY" UNDER FIRE, 1914–1918. London: Constable, 1939, 293 pp.
Review of naval actions of cruisers among all powers during World War I; details on the battles of Coronel and the Falklands; praise for Fisher for facilitating the dispatch of two battle cruisers in time to participate in the British victory at the Falklands.

544   Danchev, Alex, ed. A MATTER OF LIFE AND DEATH: INTERNATIONAL PERSPECTIVES ON THE FALKLANDS CONFLICT. London: n.p., forthcoming 1992.

To be the published proceedings of an international conference, "The Falklands Conflict," held at the University of Keele, September 1990, and including presentations by Sir Rex Hunt, former governor of the Falklands, Sir Jeremy Moore, commander of land forces, and Sir Anthony Parsons, British representative to the U.N.; other contributors included American and Argentine presenters.

545   Destefani, Laurio Hedelvio. LAS MALVINAS EN LA EPOCA HISPANA, 1600–1811. [THE MALVINAS DURING THE SPANISH ERA, 1600–1811]. Buenos Aires: Corregidor, 1981, 424 pp.

Elaborate and detailed review of the period of Spanish interest and activity related to the Falklands/Malvinas Islands including numerous documents supporting Spanish claims.

546   Destefani, Laurio Hedelvio. MANUAL DE LAS MALVINAS: DESDE 1501 A 1983. [HANDBOOK ON THE MALVINAS, 1501–1983]. Buenos Aires: Corregidor, 1984, 244 pp.

This prolific writer has assembled a comprehensive summary of Spanish and Argentine claims and positions from the earliest exploration to after the Falklands/Malvinas campaign; the bibliography listed twelve items by Destefani.

547   Dickinson, A. B. "A History of Sealing in the Falkland Islands and Dependencies, 1764–1972." Ph.D. diss., Cambridge, 1986.

Whaling and sealing were prominent occupations of the South Atlantic region for two centuries; the Falklands/Malvinas was a center of these endeavors.

548   Gray, Edwyn. THE DEVIL'S DEVICE: ROBERT WHITEHEAD AND THE HISTORY OF THE TORPEDO. Annapolis: NIP, 1975, 1991, 320 pp.

Whitehead was a British engineer who invented the torpedo late in the nineteenth century; the weapon exerted decisive influence on naval warfare and that applied to the Falklands/Malvinas campaign; included coverage of campaign in the second edition.

549 Hills, Ann. "Anchoring the Past in the Falklands: Cross Currents." HISTORY TODAY, 41 (July 1991): 4–5.

The Port Stanley area was to mark several upcoming occasions: a new museum, the tenth anniversary of the campaign, the centennial of the cathedral, and the quatracentennial of discovery by John Davis in 1592.

550 Howat, Jeremy N. T., SOUTH AMERICAN PACKETS: THE BRITISH PACKET SERVICE TO BRAZIL, THE RIVER PLATE, THE WEST COAST (VIA THE STRAITS OF MAGELLAN), AND THE FALKLAND ISLANDS, 1808–1880. York: Postal History Society, 1984, 292 pp.

The primary access to the islands in the nineteenth century was the packet boats, the navy sponsoring the service during the early century and contracted packet service and various mail schooners providing service later; the connection was Montevideo.

551 Landabury, Carlos Augusto. LA GUERRE DE MALVINAS. [THE MALVINAS WAR]. Buenos Aires: Circulo Militar, 1989, 1990, 676 pp.

A comprehensive history of the campaign from the Argentine perspective; included twelve battle plans and an extensive bibliography.

552 McCart, Neil. TWENTIETH-CENTURY PASSENGER SHIPS OF THE P&O. Wellingborough: Stephens, 1985, 233 pp.

Included coverage of P&O liner, CANBERRA, which acted as a troop ship during the campaign, pp. 194–96; CANBERRA was on a world cruise and was impressed into war service when at Naples on 2 April; converted and loaded with troops for the campaign; also used to convey over 5000 Argentine prisoners home; final arrival at Southhampton on 10 July 1982.

553 THE ROAD TO WAR. British Broadcasting Corporation television series. TV Documentary, "The Falklands Conflict." London, n.d.

Forthcoming to be a four-part documentary on "The Falklands Conflict" in preparation for the tenth anniversary.

554 Strawson, John. GENTLEMEN IN KHAKI: THE BRITISH ARMY, 1890–1990. London: Secker & Warburg; London: David & Charles, 1991, 304 pp.

History of the British army; chapter "Ordered South Again," pp. 268–76, provided coverage of the campaign including details of the various landings and operations of the commandos and "Para" forces; curiously, Correlli Barnett [22], the standard historian of the army, was not in the bibliography, pp. 285–86.

INDEX

Note: Items that appear frequently throughout this book, such as Great Britain, Argentina, and Falklands/Malvinas, are not indexed. Part II, the annotated bibliography, is also not indexed.

ABOUT THE AUTHOR

EUGENE L. RASOR is a Professor of History at Emory & Henry College. He has written extensively on British naval affairs. Among his publications are *Reform in the Royal Navy, British Naval History Since 1815* and *The Battle of Jutland* (Greenwood Press, 1991).